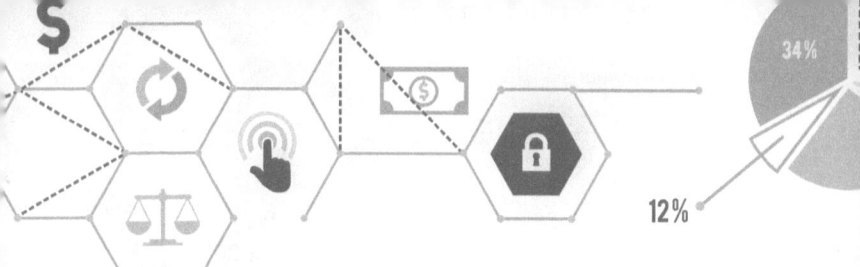

SENSE X©

Unlock Your Sense X©,
Unlock Your Financial Future

DR PRATEEP V PHILIP, IPS, PhD

Queen's Awardee for Innovation

Chennai • Bangalore

CLEVER FOX PUBLISHING
Chennai, India

Published by CLEVER FOX PUBLISHING 2024
Copyright © Dr Prateep V Philip, Queen's Awardee 2024

All Rights Reserved.
ISBN: 978-93-67074-30-5

This book has been published with all reasonable efforts taken to make the material error-free after the consent of the author. No part of this book shall be used, reproduced in any manner whatsoever without written permission from the author, except in the case of brief quotations embodied in critical articles and reviews.

The Author of this book is solely responsible and liable for its content including but not limited to the views, representations, descriptions, statements, information, opinions and references ["Content"]. The Content of this book shall not constitute or be construed or deemed to reflect the opinion or expression of the Publisher or Editor. Neither the Publisher nor Editor endorse or approve the Content of this book or guarantee the reliability, accuracy or completeness of the Content published herein and do not make any representations or warranties of any kind, express or implied, including but not limited to the implied warranties of merchantability, fitness for a particular purpose. The Publisher and Editor shall not be liable whatsoever for any errors, omissions, whether such errors or omissions result from negligence, accident, or any other cause or claims for loss or damages of any kind, including without limitation, indirect or consequential loss or damage arising out of use, inability to use, or about the reliability, accuracy or sufficiency of the information contained in this book.

*Dedicated to the Almighty who is the source
of all wisdom and the One who gives
the ability to produce wealth*

"Give a portion to seven, and also to eight; for thou knowest not what evil shall be upon the earth."

– Ecclesiastes 11:2

CONTENTS

Foreword .... *ix*
Preface .... *xiii*
Acknowledgements .... *xvii*

1. Sense X©: The Key to Financial Intelligence and Acumen 1
2. A. Analyze Expenditure and Income Regularly 8
3. B. Build and Maintain an Emergency Fund 12
4. C. Control Debt and Manage Liabilities Effectively 16
5. D. Diversify Investments to Mitigate Risk 20
6. E. Evaluate Financial Decisions Based on Long-Term Goals 24
7. F. Foster a Habit of Saving and Investing Regularly 29
8. G. Grow Financial Knowledge Through Continuous Learning 33
9. H. Have a Clear Understanding of Financial Terms and Concepts 37

Contents

10. I. Invest in Assets that Generate Passive Income 42
11. J. Justify Expenses Based on Their Value and Necessity 47
12. K. Keeping Track of Financial Transactions and Statements: The Key to Financial Health 51
13. L. Leveraging Tax-Saving Strategies to Optimize Returns 55
14. M. Minimize Unnecessary Expenses to Maximize Savings 59
15. N. Nurture a Mindset of Frugality and Resourcefulness 63
16. O. Optimize Spending by Prioritizing Needs Over Wants 67
17. P. Plan for Retirement and Create a Sustainable Income Stream 71
18. Q. Question Financial Advice and Seek Multiple Perspectives 76
19. R. Research and Understand Investment Opportunities Before Committing 80
20. S. Set Achievable Financial Goals and Milestones 84
21. T. Take Calculated Risks for Potential Financial Growth 88

22. U. Utilize Budgeting Tools and Techniques Effectively 92
23. V. Value Long-Term Financial Stability Over Short-Term Gains 96
24. W. Work Towards Building Multiple Streams of Income 101
25. X. X-Ray Your Financial Portfolio for Weaknesses and Areas of Improvement 106
26. Y. Yield to Prudent Financial Habits and Disciplined Money Management 111
27. Z. Zero in on Financial Independence and Wealth-Building Strategies 116
28. The Digital Battlefield - Scams, Schemes, and the Power of Sense X© 120

Annexure *128*
Testimonials *133*
Other Books by the Author *137*

FOREWORD

*W*hen Dr Philip asked to write the foreword, I was thinking what I can write that will add value to the concept of Sense X©. The thought that came to my mind relates to the Bhagwad Gita. Almost all the readers of this Epic would be familiar with the same and I am sure a lot many like yours truly would have struggled to fully understand the original version - at least I have. Till I came across the book "Gita" by Devdutt Patnaik. The way he has explained the Gita in his book thru 18 chapters of values immediately made a connect. This is what I find relatable to the concept of Sense X©. Financial literacy is an essential aspect that every individual should learn and understand as it is one sure way of gaining one's independence. In the life of Warren Buffet, he started understanding and learning the concept of finance at the age of 10/11 and he felt that was late. The challenge most people face is that the way it is explained is filled with mathematical jargon like the "rule of 72" and 50/30/20 for needs, wants and savings. All this starts to intimidate people.

Foreword

This book has really tried to bring the mathematical concepts to a common sense level - basically explaining the concepts in a language that a common man/ woman can understand.

As readers will relate to the proverb "a penny saved is a penny earned"- basically through the chapters Dr Philip has tried to explain how earning can be amplified- by creating diverse sources of income, how savings can be amplified through better grasp of your risk profile and how expenditure can be minimised by creating a proper record of what how and where you spend.

He has used his acumen of years spent in forces, in domains like intelligence and brought the same to the financial world emphasising a very essential thread between the two streams- that of discipline.

Towards the end he has tried to create awareness on the current malaise of cyber crime. In summary the the most valuable contribution of the author and this book is the introduction for the very first time, the idea of financial intelligence (FI) on par with IQ and EQ. That it is captioned as Sense X© makes it universally more memorable, relatable and easily understood by any person. An instrument or comprehensive questionnaire made available at the end of the book enables anyone to assess their journey in managing their finance from time to time.

In conclusion, I would again like to remind the readers of a behaviour pattern of Warren Buffet. His favourite and most regular breakfast is McDonald's- but depending on how his portfolio of investment is performing his wife gives him 2.69, 2.95 or 3.17 - yes, the exact amount for the kind of BREAKFAST he can order!

I guess that should be an inspiration for all of us to delve into this book with gusto!

Mr Rahul Chawla

Mr. Rahul Chawla till July 2024 was a Managing Director and Head of Financial Sponsor Financing, Asia at Deutsche Bank. He holds a Masters Degree in Business Administration from Indian Institute of Management, Calcutta.

PREFACE

*I*n an increasingly complex world, financial success is no longer just a matter of knowledge or skill; it demands a heightened sense of awareness, intuition, and strategic foresight—what I call "Sense X©." This book, Sense X©: Unlock Your Sense X©, Unlock Your Financial Future, is not just a guide; it is a journey into understanding and mastering the hidden forces that drive financial decisions and shape our financial destinies.

Many people approach finances with a limited perspective, focusing solely on numbers, data, and traditional strategies. However, true financial empowerment goes beyond these tangible elements. It requires tapping into a deeper level of perception—your Sense X©—that allows you to see opportunities where others see obstacles, to anticipate shifts in the market before they happen, and to make decisions with clarity and confidence even in uncertain times.

Preface

Throughout my career, I've observed that the most successful individuals aren't always the ones with the most resources or the best education. Rather, they are the ones who have honed their Sense X©, aligning their financial strategies with their unique strengths, values, and vision. This book is designed to help you do the same.

Sense X© is about breaking free from conventional thinking and embracing a holistic approach to wealth-building. It integrates insights from psychology, economics, and personal development, offering practical tools and exercises to awaken your financial intuition and apply it to real-world scenarios.

As you read through these pages, you will discover how to:

- Identify and overcome the psychological barriers that hold you back from financial success.
- Develop a sharper financial intuition to recognize and seize hidden opportunities.
- Build a personalized financial strategy that reflects your true potential and aspirations.

Whether you are just starting your financial journey or looking to elevate your current success to new heights, Sense X© is your key to unlocking a prosperous future. I invite you to embrace this journey with an open mind and a willingness to challenge your current beliefs about money and success. Your financial future is not just a matter of chance—it's something you can actively shape by unlocking the power of your Sense X©.

Welcome to a new era of financial empowerment.

Prateep V Philip
26/08/2024

ACKNOWLEDGMENTS

Writing Sense X has been a journey filled with inspiration, learning, and collaboration. This book would not have been possible without the support and encouragement of many remarkable individuals.

First and foremost, I extend my deepest gratitude to my family, whose unwavering belief in me provided the foundation for this work. Your love, patience, and constant support have been my greatest source of strength. Specific thanks to daughters Nimisha and Nishala for giving critical feedback and suggestions to design the cover.

To my friends and colleagues, thank you for your insightful feedback, late-night brainstorming sessions, and for always pushing me to think bigger and better. Your contributions have been invaluable, and I am truly grateful for your continued support. A big thanks to Mr Rahul Chawla for the thoughtful Foreword written at very short notice. Grateful also to Mr Kumar Vaidyanathan, Mr Madana Kumar, Mr P C R Suresh, Mr Osama Manzar, Mr Sukumar Samuel, Prof Thillai Rajan for their apt endorsements for the book.

Acknowledgments

A special thank you to the cybersecurity experts and financial advisors like Mr Sukumar Samuel and Rajkumar PR (of Fortune Investment Services Pvt Ltd) who generously shared their knowledge and experiences. Your insights have helped shape the content of this book and made it a practical guide for readers looking to protect their financial future.

To Miss Sumitha Menon and the entire team at Clever Fox Publishing, your meticulous attention to detail and thoughtful suggestions have elevated this book to new heights. Thank you for fast tracking the entire design and publication process to bring out an impeccable product in record time.

I also want to acknowledge the countless individuals who have bravely shared their stories of facing online scams. Your experiences serve as a powerful reminder of the importance of vigilance and the need for greater awareness in the digital age. Their names have been changed to protect their identity.

Finally, to my readers—thank you for trusting me to guide you on this journey. It is my hope that Sense X empowers you to navigate the complexities of the digital and finance world with confidence and clarity.

With heartfelt appreciation,

Prateep V Philip

CHAPTER 1

SENSE X©: THE KEY TO FINANCIAL INTELLIGENCE AND ACUMEN

Sense X© represents a new concept in the realm of finance, synonymous with financial intelligence and acumen. In this chapter, we will explore the significance of Sense X©, its importance in navigating the complexities of personal finance, and provide examples, case studies, anecdotes, and real-life stories to illustrate its significance in achieving financial success.

Understanding Sense X©

Sense X© goes beyond traditional financial literacy to encompass a holistic understanding of personal finance, including knowledge, intuition, and practical skills needed to make informed financial decisions. It involves the ability to assess financial situations, identify opportunities and risks, and navigate complex financial landscapes with confidence and clarity.

Why Sense X© Matters:

1. Empowerment: Sense X© empowers individuals to take control of their financial lives, make informed decisions, and achieve their financial goals with confidence.
2. Resilience: Sense X© equips individuals with the tools and mindset needed to navigate financial challenges, adapt to changing circumstances, and bounce back from setbacks with resilience.
3. Opportunity Identification: Sense X© enables individuals to recognize opportunities for wealth creation, financial growth, and personal fulfillment, allowing them to capitalize on emerging trends and market opportunities.

Examples and Case Studies of Sense X© in Action

Case Study 1: Entrepreneurial Success with Sense X©

Sarah, an entrepreneur with a keen sense of financial intelligence, identified a gap in the market for sustainable fashion accessories. Leveraging her understanding of consumer trends and market demand, Sarah launched a successful e-commerce business specializing in eco-friendly handbags and accessories. Through strategic pricing, marketing, and product differentiation, Sarah's business thrived, generating substantial revenue and profit. Her Sense X© allowed her to navigate the competitive landscape of the fashion industry, capitalize on emerging trends, and build a profitable business from the ground up.

Case Study 2: Investment Success through Sense X©

Mark, an investor with a strong sense of financial acumen, recognized the potential of renewable energy as a lucrative investment opportunity. With thorough research and analysis, Mark identified promising companies in the renewable energy sector and strategically allocated a portion of his investment portfolio to these stocks. As the renewable energy industry experienced rapid growth and innovation, Mark's investments yielded significant returns, outperforming the broader market. His Sense X© enabled him to identify promising investment opportunities, assess risk factors, and capitalize on trends that aligned with his long-term financial goals.

Anecdotes and Real-Life Stories Demonstrating Sense X©

Anecdote 1: Strategic Debt Management

David, a financially savvy individual with a strong sense of financial intelligence, strategically managed his debt to optimize his financial situation. By prioritizing high- interest debt repayment, consolidating loans, and negotiating lower interest rates, David minimized interest costs and accelerated his journey towards debt freedom.

His Sense X© enabled him to devise a comprehensive debt repayment strategy that aligned with his financial goals, ultimately achieving financial independence and freedom from debt.

Anecdote 2: Lifestyle Optimization

Emily, a young professional with a sense of financial acumen, practiced lifestyle optimization to maximize her financial resources. By prioritizing needs over wants, practicing frugality, and seeking out cost-effective alternatives, Emily was able to live comfortably within her means while saving and investing for the future. Her Sense X© allowed her to make intentional choices about her spending habits, prioritize long- term financial goals, and achieve financial security and stability at a young age.

Practical Strategies for Developing Sense X©

1. Continuous Learning: Stay informed about financial trends, concepts, and strategies through reading, research, and education.
2. Critical Thinking: Develop critical thinking skills to evaluate financial information, assess risks, and make informed decisions.
3. Practical Experience: Gain practical experience through real-world application of financial concepts, such as budgeting, investing, and risk management.
4. Seeking Advice: Seek advice from financial professionals, mentors, and peers to gain insights and perspectives on complex financial issues.

Conclusion

Sense X© represents a holistic approach to financial intelligence and acumen, encompassing knowledge, intuition, and practical skills needed to navigate the complexities of personal finance. By developing Sense X©, individuals can empower themselves to make informed financial decisions, capitalize on opportunities, and achieve their financial goals with confidence and clarity. Remember, cultivating Sense X© is an ongoing journey that requires dedication, curiosity, and a commitment to lifelong learning and growth.

Here are the 26 principles of financial acumen, called Sense X©, alphabetically arranged from A to Z:

A. Analyze expenses and income regularly.
B. Build and maintain an emergency fund.
C. Control debt and manage liabilities effectively.
D. Diversify investments to mitigate risk.
E. Evaluate financial decisions based on long-term goals.
F. Foster a habit of saving and investing regularly.
G. Grow financial knowledge through continuous learning.
H. Have a clear understanding of financial terms and concepts.
I. Invest in assets that generate passive income.
J. Justify expenses based on their value and necessity.
K. Keep track of financial transactions and statements.
L. Leverage tax-saving strategies to optimize returns.
M. Minimize unnecessary expenses to maximize savings.
N. Nurture a mindset of frugality and resourcefulness.
O. Optimize spending by prioritizing needs over wants.
P. Plan for retirement and create a sustainable income stream.
Q. Question financial advice and seek multiple perspectives.
R. Research and understand investment opportunities before committing.

S. Set achievable financial goals and milestones.
T. Take calculated risks for potential financial growth.
U. Utilize budgeting tools and techniques effectively.
V. Value long-term financial stability over short-term gains.
W. Work towards building multiple streams of income.
X. X-ray your financial portfolio for weaknesses and areas of improvement.
Y. Yield to prudent financial habits and disciplined money management.
Z. Zero in on financial independence and wealth-building strategies.

CHAPTER 2

A. ANALYZE EXPENDITURE AND INCOME REGULARLY

Introduction:

Analyzing expenditure and income regularly is the cornerstone of financial acumen. By understanding where money is coming from and where it is going, individuals can make informed decisions to improve their financial health. In this chapter, we will delve into why regular analysis is crucial, provide practical examples, share anecdotes, and discuss tools for effective analysis.

Why Analyze Expenditure and Income?

Regular analysis of expenditure and income offers several benefits:

A. Analyze Expenditure and Income Regularly

1. Financial Awareness: It provides insight into spending patterns and income sources, fostering a deeper understanding of one's financial situation.
2. Identifying Trends: Tracking expenses and income over time reveals trends, such as seasonal fluctuations or changes in earning capacity, enabling proactive adjustments.
3. Budget Optimization: Armed with data, individuals can identify areas of overspending or opportunities to allocate resources more effectively, optimizing their budget.
4. Goal Alignment: Analysis helps align financial habits with long-term goals, ensuring that spending and saving decisions contribute to desired outcomes.

Examples and Anecdotes:

1. Tracking Daily Expenses: Sarah, a young professional, decided to track her daily expenses for a month. She was surprised to discover that she spent a significant portion of her income on dining out. By analyzing this data, she adjusted her habits and saved enough to start investing in a retirement fund.
2. Monitoring Income Streams: John, a freelancer, analyzed his income sources quarterly. He noticed that one client consistently provided the majority of his earnings. Concerned about dependence on a single

source, he diversified his client base, reducing risk and stabilizing his income.

3. Identifying Hidden Costs: David leased a car without fully understanding the total cost of ownership. By analyzing his monthly expenses, he realized that maintenance, insurance, and fuel expenses were higher than anticipated. Armed with this knowledge, he reconsidered his transportation options, ultimately saving money.

Tools of Analysis:

1. Budgeting Apps: Apps like Mint, Fi Money and YNAB (You Need a Budget) sync with bank accounts to automatically categorize expenses and track income, providing users with comprehensive financial snapshots.
2. Spreadsheets: Excel or Google Sheets offer customizable templates for tracking expenses and income. Users can create personalized budgets, visualize data through charts, and set alerts for overspending.
3. Receipt Scanners: Apps like Receipts by Wave or Expensify allow users to scan receipts and categorize expenses on the go, streamlining the process of recording expenditures.
4. Cash Flow Statements: Creating monthly or quarterly cash flow statements helps visualize inflows and

outflows of cash, facilitating analysis of income sources and expenditure patterns.

Conclusion:

Regular analysis of expenditure and income is not merely a financial chore but a strategic practice that empowers individuals to make informed decisions about their money. By cultivating this habit and leveraging tools for analysis, individuals can achieve greater financial stability, align their actions with their goals, and pave the way for long-term prosperity.

CHAPTER 3

B. BUILD AND MAINTAIN AN EMERGENCY FUND

Introduction:

An emergency fund serves as a financial safety net, providing peace of mind and protection against unforeseen expenses or sudden income loss. In this chapter, we will explore the importance of building and maintaining an emergency fund, share real- life examples, anecdotes, and strategies for creating and managing this essential financial buffer.

Why Build and Maintain an Emergency Fund?

1. Financial Stability: An emergency fund cushions against financial shocks, such as medical emergencies, car repairs, or job loss, preventing individuals from falling into debt or depleting savings meant for other purposes.

2. Reduced Stress: Knowing that funds are readily available in case of emergencies alleviates stress and anxiety, allowing individuals to focus on solutions rather than worrying about financial fallout.
3. Avoiding Debt: Without an emergency fund, unexpected expenses often lead to reliance on high-interest loans or credit cards, exacerbating financial strain. A well-funded emergency fund mitigates the need for borrowing.
4. Opportunity Seizing: Having a financial cushion empowers individuals to seize opportunities, such as investing in a promising venture or pursuing further education, without fear of jeopardizing their financial security.

Examples and Anecdotes:

1. The Story of Emily: Emily diligently saved a portion of her income each month, gradually building her emergency fund. When her car broke down unexpectedly, she was grateful to have funds readily available to cover the repair costs, avoiding financial stress and disruption to her life.
2. John experienced a sudden job loss during a downturn in his industry. Thanks to his well-funded emergency fund, he could cover his living expenses while searching for a new job, maintaining financial stability for himself and his family until he secured employment.

3. Medical Emergency: Sara's elderly parent had an unexpected medical emergency that required costly treatment. Sara's emergency fund provided the necessary funds to cover medical bills without dipping into her long-term savings or retirement funds, ensuring financial security for both her parent and herself.

Strategies for Building and Maintaining an Emergency Fund:

1. Set Clear Savings Goals: Determine the desired size of your emergency fund based on your monthly expenses, income stability, and individual circumstances. Aim to save enough to cover three to six months' worth of living expenses.
2. Automate Savings: Set up automatic transfers from your paycheck or checking account to a dedicated emergency fund account. Treating savings as a non-negotiable expense increases consistency and discipline.
3. Cut Expenses: Review your budget and identify areas where you can reduce spending to accelerate emergency fund growth. Redirecting funds from non-essential expenses towards savings reinforces financial prudence.
4. Keep Funds Accessible: While it is essential to maintain liquidity, consider keeping emergency funds

in a separate savings account or money market account that offers competitive interest rates and easy access when needed.

Conclusion:

Building and maintaining an emergency fund is a fundamental aspect of financial planning that provides stability, security, and peace of mind. By prioritizing savings, leveraging examples and anecdotes, and implementing effective strategies, individuals can safeguard themselves against unforeseen financial challenges and pave the way for a more secure financial future.

CHAPTER 4

C. CONTROL DEBT AND MANAGE LIABILITIES EFFECTIVELY

Introduction:

Debt can be a double-edged sword, offering opportunities for financial growth while also posing risks to long-term financial health. In this chapter, we will explore the importance of controlling debt and managing liabilities effectively, sharing practical examples, anecdotes, and tools to empower individuals in their journey towards financial stability.

Why Control Debt and Manage Liabilities?

1. Financial Freedom: Excessive debt can limit financial freedom, tying up income in interest payments and

C. Control Debt and Manage Liabilities Effectively

reducing disposable income for essential expenses, savings, and investments.

2. Risk Mitigation: High levels of debt increase vulnerability to financial shocks, such as job loss or unexpected expenses, amplifying stress and hindering recovery efforts.
3. Interest Savings: By managing liabilities effectively, individuals can minimize interest payments, redirecting funds towards wealth-building activities such as savings, investments, or debt reduction.
4. Creditworthiness: Responsible debt management improves creditworthiness, enabling access to favorable loan terms, lower interest rates, and increased financial flexibility in the future.

Examples and Anecdotes:

1. The Tale of Mike's Credit Card Debt: Mike accumulated significant credit card debt during his college years, splurging on non-essential items and neglecting to budget effectively. High-interest payments quickly spiraled out of control, hampering his ability to achieve his financial goals. Through disciplined budgeting and prioritizing debt repayment, Mike regained control of his finances and eventually achieved debt freedom.
2. Sara's Student Loan Journey: Sara carefully evaluated her student loan options before pursuing higher education, opting for federal loans with favorable

terms and repayment options. After graduation, she diligently repaid her loans while also prioritizing savings and investments. By managing her liabilities effectively, Sara maintained financial stability and achieved her long-term goals without being burdened by excessive debt.

3. The Mortgage Dilemma: John and Emily were excited to purchase their first home but were cautious about taking on too much debt. They researched various mortgage options, opting for a fixed-rate mortgage with manageable monthly payments. By staying within their budget and avoiding unnecessary expenses, they successfully navigated homeownership without becoming overwhelmed by debt.

Tools for Managing Debt and Liabilities:

1. Debt Snowball or Avalanche Method: Utilize debt repayment strategies such as the debt snowball (paying off debts from smallest to largest) or the debt avalanche (prioritizing debts with the highest interest rates) to accelerate debt repayment and minimize interest costs.
2. Budgeting Apps: Track expenses, set spending limits, and allocate funds towards debt repayment using budgeting apps like Mint or YNAB.
3. Credit Monitoring Services: Monitor your credit score and receive alerts about changes in your credit report using services like Sibil, Credit Karma or Experian

C. Control Debt and Manage Liabilities Effectively

to ensure accuracy and identify potential areas for improvement.

4. Loan Refinancing: Explore opportunities to refinance high-interest debt, such as credit cards or student loans, into lower-interest alternatives to reduce monthly payments and overall interest costs.

Conclusion:

Controlling debt and managing liabilities effectively are essential components of financial well-being. By prioritizing debt repayment, making informed financial decisions, and leveraging tools for debt management, individuals can reduce financial stress, improve creditworthiness, and pave the way for long-term financial success.

CHAPTER 5

D. DIVERSIFY INVESTMENTS TO MITIGATE RISK

Introduction:

Diversification is a fundamental principle of investing aimed at reducing risk by spreading investments across different asset classes, industries, and geographic regions. In this chapter, we will explore the importance of diversifying investments, provide practical examples, anecdotes, and highlight tools to help individuals implement effective diversification strategies.

Why Diversify Investments?

1. Risk Reduction: Diversification helps mitigate the impact of market volatility and specific risks associated with individual investments. By spreading investments across different assets, investors can minimize the impact of adverse events on their overall portfolio.

D. Diversify Investments to Mitigate Risk

2. Enhanced Returns: Diversification can potentially enhance long-term returns by capturing gains from multiple sources of growth while reducing the likelihood of significant losses from any single investment.

3. Stability and Resilience: A diversified portfolio is better positioned to withstand economic downturns or industry-specific challenges, maintaining stability and resilience in the face of market fluctuations.

4. Asset Allocation: Diversification allows investors to align their portfolios with their risk tolerance, investment objectives, and time horizon, creating a balanced mix of assets tailored to their individual needs.

Examples and Anecdotes:

1. The Story of Jane's Portfolio: Jane invested all her savings in a single stock that had performed well historically. However, when the company faced financial difficulties, the stock plummeted, resulting in a significant loss for Jane. Had she diversified her investments across multiple stocks, bonds, and other asset classes, the impact of this downturn would have been mitigated.

2. The Benefits of Sector Diversification: Tom diversified his investment portfolio by allocating funds across various sectors such as technology, healthcare, and

consumer goods. While some sectors experienced downturns during economic downturns, others remained resilient, resulting in a balanced overall performance for Tom's portfolio.

3. Geographic Diversification in Action: Sarah invested solely in her local real estate market, believing it offered the best opportunities for growth. However, when the local market experienced a downturn, Sarah suffered significant losses. By diversifying her real estate investments across different regions or investing in global real estate funds, Sarah could have reduced her exposure to local market risks.

Tools for Diversifying Investments:

1. Exchange-Traded Funds (ETFs) and Mutual Funds: ETFs and mutual funds provide instant diversification by pooling investors' funds and investing in a diversified portfolio of assets, including stocks, bonds, and commodities. By investing a major part of the fairly large corpus I got as retirement benefits in selected Mutual Funds with high CAGR of 20 to 30 percent, I have not only built up that capital but have an additional source of income post-retirement and additional benefit is that the tax on such long term capital is not clubbed with total income even if one is in the highest tax bracket. Mutual funds are quite liquid and whenever I need funds for expenses, I

liquidate any profit on the capital and get the credit to my account in three to five days.

2. Asset Allocation Tools: Online platforms and investment tools offer asset allocation calculators and portfolio analysis tools to help investors determine the optimal mix of asset classes based on their risk tolerance and investment goals.
3. Robo-Advisors: Robo-advisors utilize algorithms to create and manage diversified investment portfolios tailored to investors' preferences and goals, offering a hands-off approach to diversification.
4. Global Investment Platforms: Access global markets and diversify investments across different countries and regions using online investment platforms that offer international trading capabilities.

Conclusion:

Diversifying investments is a key strategy for reducing risk and achieving long-term financial success. By spreading investments across different asset classes, sectors, and geographic regions, investors can enhance portfolio stability, resilience, and potential returns. Leveraging tools for diversification and learning from real-life examples, individuals can build well-balanced investment portfolios that withstand market volatility and deliver sustainable growth over time.

CHAPTER 6

E. EVALUATE FINANCIAL DECISIONS BASED ON LONG-TERM GOALS

Introduction:

Evaluating financial decisions through the lens of long-term goals is crucial for fostering financial success and security. In this chapter, we will delve into the significance of aligning decisions with long-term objectives, provide practical examples, anecdotes, and introduce tools to assist individuals in making informed choices that support their future aspirations.

Why Evaluate Financial Decisions with Long-Term Goals in Mind?

1. Strategic Planning: Considering long-term goals helps individuals make strategic decisions that contribute to

their overall financial well-being, ensuring actions are purposeful and aligned with desired outcomes.
2. Persistence and Motivation: Long-term goals serve as a source of motivation and persistence, encouraging individuals to stay committed to their financial plans despite short-term challenges or setbacks.
3. Resource Allocation: Evaluating decisions in the context of long-term goals facilitates efficient resource allocation, directing funds towards activities that have the greatest impact on achieving desired objectives.
4. Adaptability: Long-term goals provide a framework for adapting to changing circumstances, allowing individuals to adjust strategies and priorities while maintaining a clear focus on their ultimate aspirations.

Examples and Anecdotes:

1. Retirement Planning: Emily and James envisioned a comfortable retirement that would allow them to pursue their passions and travel the world. They evaluated their financial decisions, such as retirement savings contributions and investment strategies, based on their long-term goal of financial independence. This approach ensured they remained on track to realize their retirement dreams.
2. Homeownership: Sarah and David aspired to own a home where they could raise a family and create lasting memories. They evaluated various factors, including

mortgage options, down payment requirements, and affordability, in light of their long-term goal of homeownership. By prioritizing savings and making informed decisions, they successfully achieved their dream of purchasing a home.

3. Education Funding: John and Lisa valued education and wanted to provide their children with the best opportunities for academic success. They evaluated financial decisions, such as college savings contributions and investment strategies, based on their long-term goal of funding their children's education. This perspective guided them to establish college savings accounts and make regular contributions to ensure they could afford their children's educational expenses.

4. Jay, an auditor by profession failed to renew medical insurance policy for his spouse and as a result ended up spending a fortune when she had to be hospitalised frequently. Taking suitable cash-free medical and other insurance policies helps to provide a sense of security in times of such crisis. Insurance helps to also avail many tax benefits and when linked with savings schemes to provide for contingent expenditure, like children's education.

Tools for Evaluating Financial Decisions:

1. Goal Setting Worksheets: Utilize goal setting worksheets and templates to articulate long-term financial objectives, such as retirement savings targets, education funding goals, or debt repayment plans.
2. Financial Planning Software: Explore financial planning software or apps that enable users to input long-term goals, track progress, and simulate the impact of different financial decisions on achieving those goals.
3. Cost-Benefit Analysis Framework: Apply a cost-benefit analysis framework to evaluate financial decisions, weighing the short-term costs against the long-term benefits and assessing alignment with overarching goals.
4. Professional Guidance: Seek advice from financial advisors or planners who can provide personalized recommendations and help evaluate financial decisions within the context of long-term objectives, taking into account individual circumstances and preferences.

Conclusion:

Evaluating financial decisions through the prism of long-term goals is essential for building a secure financial future. By anchoring decisions in broader aspirations, individuals can prioritize activities that contribute most significantly to their overall well-being, navigate challenges with resilience, and remain focused on realizing their long-term dreams. Leveraging tools for goal setting and decision-making, individuals can make informed choices that support their vision for the future and pave the way for lasting financial success.

CHAPTER 7

F. FOSTER A HABIT OF SAVING AND INVESTING REGULARLY

Introduction:

Developing a habit of saving and investing regularly is key to achieving financial stability and building long-term wealth. In this chapter, we will explore the importance of fostering this habit, provide practical examples, anecdotes, and discuss strategies to help individuals incorporate regular saving and investing into their financial routines.

Why Foster a Habit of Saving and Investing Regularly?

1. Building Wealth: Regular saving and investing allow individuals to accumulate wealth gradually over time, harnessing the power of compound interest to grow their assets exponentially.

2. Financial Security: Saving regularly creates a financial safety net, providing funds for emergencies, unexpected expenses, or periods of reduced income, thereby enhancing financial resilience.
3. Goal Achievement: Consistent saving and investing enable individuals to work towards their financial goals, whether it is buying a home, funding education, or retiring comfortably, by steadily accumulating the necessary resources.
4. Discipline and Self-Control: Cultivating a habit of saving and investing instills discipline and self-control, fostering responsible financial behavior and reducing the temptation to overspend or indulge in impulsive purchases.

Examples and Anecdotes:

1. The Story of Maria's Retirement Fund: Maria started saving a portion of her income regularly in her early twenties, contributing to her employer-sponsored retirement account and a separate investment portfolio. Over the years, her disciplined approach to saving and investing allowed her retirement fund to grow significantly, providing her with financial security and peace of mind as she approached retirement age.
2. John's Emergency Fund: John established a habit of setting aside a portion of his income every month into an emergency fund. When he unexpectedly lost his

job during a recession, his emergency fund provided a buffer, allowing him to cover his expenses while he searched for a new job without resorting to debt or tapping into his long-term savings.
3. Sarah's College Savings Plan: Sarah and her husband committed to saving a fixed amount of money each month towards their children's college education. By consistently contributing to a college savings plan, they were able to accumulate a substantial sum by the time their children reached college age, alleviating the financial burden of tuition and expenses.

Strategies for Fostering a Habit of Saving and Investing:

1. Set Clear Goals: Define specific savings and investment goals, such as building an emergency fund, saving for retirement, or achieving a financial milestone, to provide motivation and direction for your saving efforts.
2. Automate Savings: Set up automatic transfers from your paycheck or checking account to designated savings or investment accounts to ensure consistent contributions without the need for manual intervention. For example, for more than ten years, every month a fixed sum is paid into my Public Provident Fund.

3. Pay Yourself First: Prioritize saving and investing by allocating a portion of your income towards these goals before paying for other expenses, treating savings as a non-negotiable expense.
4. Track Progress: Monitor your savings and investment accounts regularly to track progress towards your goals, celebrate milestones, and adjust your savings rate or investment strategy as needed.

Conclusion:

Fostering a habit of saving and investing regularly is a cornerstone of financial success. By committing to consistent saving and investing, individuals can build wealth, achieve financial goals, and secure their future. Drawing inspiration from successful investors and implementing practical strategies, individuals can cultivate a mindset of financial responsibility and set themselves on the path to long-term financial well-being.

CHAPTER 8

G. GROW FINANCIAL KNOWLEDGE THROUGH CONTINUOUS LEARNING

Introduction:

In the ever-evolving landscape of personal finance, continuous learning is essential for making informed decisions and achieving financial success. In this chapter, weâll explore the importance of growing financial knowledge, provide practical examples, anecdotes, and discuss strategies to foster a habit of lifelong learning in matters of finance.

Why Grow Financial Knowledge Through Continuous Learning?

1. Empowerment: Financial knowledge empowers individuals to take control of their financial lives, make

informed decisions, and navigate complex financial situations with confidence.
2. Adaptability: Continuous learning enables individuals to stay abreast of changes in financial markets, regulations, and economic trends, allowing them to adapt their strategies and tactics accordingly.
3. Risk Management: A deeper understanding of financial concepts and principles equips individuals to identify and mitigate risks, whether it is managing debt, investing in the stock market, or planning for retirement.
4. Opportunity Identification: Financial knowledge opens doors to opportunities for wealth creation, whether it is exploring new investment avenues, optimizing tax strategies, or launching entrepreneurial ventures.

Examples and Anecdotes:

1. The Journey of Alex: Alex recognized the importance of financial literacy early in his career and embarked on a journey of continuous learning. He devoured books, attended seminars, and sought mentorship from seasoned investors. Armed with knowledge, he navigated market downturns, capitalized on investment opportunities, and ultimately achieved financial independence.

2. Emily's Investment Education: Emily inherited a sum of money from her grandparents but lacked the knowledge to manage it effectively. Determined to learn, she enrolled in online courses, joined investment clubs, and sought guidance from financial advisors. Over time, her confidence grew, and she transformed from a novice investor into a savvy wealth builder, securing her financial future in the process.
3. The Power of Networking: Sarah realized the value of networking in expanding her financial knowledge. She attended industry conferences, joined professional associations, and participated in online forums. Through networking, she connected with experts, exchanged ideas, and gained valuable insights that helped her make better financial decisions and advance her career.

Strategies for Continuous Learning in Finance:

1. Read Widely: Explore a variety of resources, including books, articles, blogs, and reputable financial publications, to gain diverse perspectives and insights into different aspects of personal finance, investing, and economics.
2. Take Courses and Workshops: Enroll in online courses, workshops, or seminars offered by reputable educational institutions, industry organizations, or

financial experts to deepen your understanding of specific topics and acquire practical skills.
3. Seek Mentorship: Identify mentors or financial advisors who can provide guidance, share their expertise, and offer personalized advice tailored to your financial goals and circumstances.
4. Stay Informed: Stay updated on financial news, market trends, and regulatory changes by following reputable sources, subscribing to newsletters, or listening to financial podcasts and webinars.

Conclusion:

Growing financial knowledge through continuous learning is essential for achieving financial success and security in today's complex world. By embracing lifelong learning, individuals can empower themselves to make informed decisions, adapt to changing circumstances, and capitalize on opportunities for wealth creation. The concept of Sense X© can help individuals get a grip on their finances and cultivate a mindset of curiosity and lifelong growth in matters of finance.

CHAPTER 9

H. HAVE A CLEAR UNDERSTANDING OF FINANCIAL TERMS AND CONCEPTS

Introduction:

A clear understanding of financial terms and concepts is crucial for making sound financial decisions and navigating the complexities of personal finance. In this chapter, we will explore the importance of financial literacy, provide practical examples of terms and concepts, share anecdotes of how they proved useful to different individuals, and discuss strategies to enhance financial knowledge.

Why Have a Clear Understanding of Financial Terms and Concepts?

1. Informed Decision-Making: Understanding financial terms and concepts empowers individuals to make informed decisions about budgeting, saving, investing, borrowing, and other financial activities.
2. Effective Communication: Clarity in financial language facilitates communication with financial professionals, advisors, and institutions, ensuring that individuals can articulate their needs, goals, and preferences accurately.
3. Risk Management: Familiarity with financial terms and concepts enables individuals to assess and mitigate risks associated with investments, loans, insurance, and other financial products or services.
4. Empowerment: Financial literacy fosters a sense of empowerment and confidence, allowing individuals to take control of their financial lives, set goals, and pursue strategies for wealth creation and financial security.

Examples of Financial Terms and Concepts:

1. Compound Interest: The concept of compound interest, where interest is calculated on both the initial principal and the accumulated interest, is fundamental to understanding the growth potential of savings and investments over time.

2. Asset Allocation: Asset allocation refers to the distribution of investments across different asset classes, such as stocks, bonds, and cash equivalents, to achieve a balance between risk and return tailored to an individual's investment objectives and risk tolerance.
3. Credit Score: A credit score is a numerical representation of an individual's creditworthiness, based on their credit history, payment behavior, outstanding debts, and other factors. A higher credit score indicates lower credit risk and may result in better loan terms and interest rates.
4. Budgeting: Budgeting involves planning and tracking income and expenses to ensure that spending aligns with financial goals and priorities. It helps individuals manage cash flow, avoid overspending, and allocate resources effectively.

Anecdotes of How Financial Literacy Was Beneficial:

1. The Power of Compound Interest: Tom understood the concept of compound interest and started investing in his retirement accounts early in his career. Over time, his investments grew substantially due to the power of compounding, providing him with a comfortable retirement nest egg. The earlier one starts in a SIP or systematic investment plan the greater the power of compounding. A small sum of even 500 dollars

invested in a SIP realises a huge fortune over three decades building into a corpus of several thousand dollars.

2. Asset Allocation for Risk Management: Sarah diversified her investment portfolio across different asset classes based on her risk tolerance and investment objectives. When the stock market experienced a downturn, the bond and cash holdings in her portfolio helped cushion the impact on her overall investment performance.

3. Improving Credit Score for Better Loan Terms: Emily learned about the importance of maintaining a good credit score and took steps to improve hers by paying bills on time, reducing credit card balances, and monitoring her credit report. When she applied for a mortgage, her improved credit score resulted in lower interest rates and saved her thousands of dollars in interest payments over the life of the loan.

Strategies for Enhancing Financial Literacy:

1. Self-Study: Take advantage of online resources, books, articles, and educational materials to learn about financial terms and concepts at your own pace.

2. Formal Education: Consider enrolling in financial literacy courses, workshops, or seminars offered by educational institutions, community organizations, or financial institutions.

3. Seek Guidance: Consult with financial advisors, planners, or mentors who can provide personalized guidance, answer questions, and help clarify financial terms and concepts.
4. Practice: Apply financial knowledge to real-life situations by creating budgets, managing investments, and making financial decisions, honing your understanding and skills over time.

Conclusion:

Having a clear understanding of financial terms and concepts is essential for navigating the complexities of personal finance and achieving financial goals. By familiarizing themselves with key concepts and adopting strategies for continuous learning, individuals can enhance their financial literacy, make informed decisions, and ultimately build a solid foundation for financial success and security.

CHAPTER 10

I. INVEST IN ASSETS THAT GENERATE PASSIVE INCOME

Introduction:

Investing in assets that generate passive income is a powerful strategy for building wealth, achieving financial freedom, and creating a sustainable source of income with minimal ongoing effort. In this chapter, we will explore the importance of passive income, provide practical examples of assets that generate passive income, share anecdotes of individuals who have successfully built passive income streams, and discuss strategies for getting started with passive investing.

Why Invest in Assets that Generate Passive Income?

1. Financial Freedom: Passive income provides a steady stream of income that can supplement or replace

earned income, allowing individuals to achieve financial independence and pursue their passions without being tied to a traditional job.

2. Diversification: Investing in assets that generate passive income diversifies income sources, reducing reliance on a single source of income and providing stability in varying economic conditions.

3. Wealth Building: Passive income streams have the potential to grow and compound over time, accelerating wealth accumulation and creating opportunities for long-term financial growth and prosperity.

4. Time Freedom: Passive income requires minimal ongoing effort once established, freeing up time for individuals to focus on other pursuits, such as spending time with family, pursuing hobbies, or exploring new ventures.

Examples of Assets that Generate Passive Income:

1. Dividend-Paying Stocks: Investing in dividend-paying stocks allows investors to earn regular income in the form of dividends, which are typically distributed quarterly or annually by publicly traded companies.

2. Rental Properties: Owning rental properties generates passive income through rental payments from tenants, providing a steady stream of cash flow while also offering potential for property appreciation over time.

Our parent's home that we (my elder sibling and I) inherited, we knocked down about ten years ago and turned it into a commercial building with much higher rents.

3. Real Estate Investment Trusts (REITs): REITs are investment vehicles that allow individuals to invest in a portfolio of income-producing real estate properties, such as commercial buildings, apartments, or shopping centers, and receive regular dividends from rental income.
4. Peer-to-Peer Lending: Peer-to-peer lending platforms enable individuals to invest in loans to borrowers and earn interest income on their investments, providing an alternative source of passive income with potentially higher returns than traditional savings accounts or bonds.

Anecdotes of Successful Passive Income Ventures:

1. The Dividend Investor: John invested in a diversified portfolio of dividend- paying stocks, focusing on companies with a history of stable dividend payments and strong financial fundamentals. Over time, the dividends from his investments grew significantly, providing him with a reliable source of passive income that covered his living expenses in retirement.

I. Invest in Assets that Generate Passive Income

2. The Real Estate Mogul: Sarah purchased several rental properties in growing markets, leveraging rental income to cover mortgage payments and generate positive cash flow. As her portfolio grew, so did her passive income, allowing her to scale her real estate investments and achieve financial independence at a relatively young age.
3. The Passive Investor: Emily diversified her investment portfolio by allocating a portion of her funds to peer-to-peer lending platforms. By lending to borrowers with solid credit profiles and earning interest income on her investments, she built a passive income stream that supplemented her salary and provided financial flexibility.

Strategies for Getting Started with Passive Investing:

1. Research and Education: Take the time to research different passive income opportunities, understand the risks and rewards associated with each investment vehicle, and educate yourself about the principles of passive investing.
2. Start Small and Diversify: Begin with a small investment in one or two passive income streams and gradually diversify your portfolio to spread risk and maximize returns over time.

3. Set Realistic Goals: Define clear financial goals for your passive income endeavors, whether it is generating additional income to cover expenses, saving for retirement, or achieving financial independence, and develop a plan to work towards those goals.
4. Monitor and Adjust: Regularly monitor the performance of your passive income investments, evaluate their contribution to your overall financial objectives, and make adjustments as needed to optimize returns and mitigate risks.

Conclusion:

Investing in assets that generate passive income is a powerful wealth-building strategy that offers financial freedom, diversification, and opportunities for long-term growth. By identifying suitable passive income opportunities, learning from examples of successful passive investors, individuals can create sustainable sources of income that support their financial goals and aspirations for the future.

CHAPTER 11

J. JUSTIFY EXPENSES BASED ON THEIR VALUE AND NECESSITY

Introduction:

Every expense incurred has an impact on one's financial health and overall well- being. Justifying expenses based on their value and necessity is essential for maintaining financial discipline, achieving financial goals, and ensuring that resources are allocated effectively. In this chapter, we will delve into the importance of evaluating expenses, provide practical examples, case studies, and discuss strategies for making informed spending decisions.

Why Justify Expenses Based on Their Value and Necessity?

1. Financial Discipline: Evaluating expenses based on their value and necessity fosters financial discipline,

helping individuals prioritize spending and avoid impulse purchases or frivolous expenditures.
2. Resource Allocation: By justifying expenses, individuals can allocate resources towards activities or purchases that align with their priorities, values, and long-term goals, maximizing the impact of their spending.
3. Budget Management: Justifying expenses enables individuals to adhere to budgetary constraints, ensuring that spending remains within sustainable limits and supporting overall financial health.
4. Goal Achievement: Aligning expenses with value and necessity facilitates progress towards financial goals, whether it is saving for a down payment on a home, funding education, or building an emergency fund, by directing funds towards activities that contribute most significantly to desired outcomes.

Examples and Case Studies:

1. The Dilemma of Dining Out:
   Scenario: Sarah enjoys dining out at restaurants several times a week, often spending a significant portion of her discretionary income on meals.
   Justification: Sarah evaluates her dining expenses based on the value they provide in terms of convenience, social interaction, and enjoyment. While she values the experience of dining out, she recognizes that it

J. Justify Expenses Based on Their Value and Necessity

may not be necessary for every meal and considers alternatives, such as meal prepping at home or choosing more budget-friendly dining options.

2. The Impulse Purchase:
   Scenario: John comes across a high-end electronic gadget that he has been eyeing for a while. Despite the hefty price tag, he decides to purchase it on impulse.
   Justification: Reflecting on the purchase, John realizes that while the gadget may provide temporary satisfaction, its value in terms of long-term utility and necessity is limited. He acknowledges that he could have allocated the funds towards more meaningful expenses, such as savings or investments, that align better with his financial goals.

3. The Subscription Trap:
   Scenario: Emily subscribes to multiple streaming services, magazine subscriptions, and online memberships without closely evaluating their value relative to their costs.
   Justification: Upon reviewing her expenses, Emily realizes that while each subscription may seem affordable individually, the cumulative cost adds up significantly over time. She assesses the value and necessity of each subscription, canceling those that provide little value or are redundant, and reallocates the savings towards activities or services that offer greater utility and fulfillment.

Strategies for Justifying Expenses:

1. Define Priorities: Identify your financial priorities, goals, and values to guide spending decisions and ensure that resources are allocated towards activities that align with your objectives.
2. Evaluate Value: Assess the value of each expense relative to its cost, considering factors such as utility, enjoyment, necessity, and long-term impact on your financial well-being.
3. Set Spending Limits: Establish spending limits or budgets for different expense categories, such as dining out, entertainment, or clothing, to ensure that spending remains within sustainable levels and supports overall financial health.
4. Practice Delayed Gratification: Adopt a habit of delaying non-essential purchases and taking time to evaluate their value and necessity before making a decision, reducing the likelihood of impulse spending and promoting mindful consumption.

Conclusion:

Justifying expenses based on their value and necessity is essential for maintaining financial discipline, achieving financial goals, and ensuring that resources are allocated effectively. By evaluating expenses thoughtfully, individuals can cultivate a mindset of mindful consumption, optimize their use of resources, and pave the way for long-term financial success and fulfillment.

CHAPTER 12

K. KEEPING TRACK OF FINANCIAL TRANSACTIONS AND STATEMENTS: THE KEY TO FINANCIAL HEALTH

*M*anaging personal finances effectively requires more than just earning money and paying bills. It involves keeping track of every financial transaction and staying informed about your financial statements. This chapter will delve into the importance of tracking financial transactions and statements, provide examples and case studies, and discuss tools and strategies to help individuals maintain financial health.

Importance of Keeping Track:

1. Financial Awareness: Tracking financial transactions and statements provides individuals with a clear picture of their income, expenses, assets, and liabilities. This

awareness is crucial for making informed decisions and maintaining financial stability.

2. Budgeting: By recording and categorizing expenses, individuals can create budgets that align with their financial goals. Tracking transactions allows them to identify areas where they may be overspending and make adjustments accordingly.
3. Detecting Errors and Fraud: Regularly monitoring financial statements helps detect errors, unauthorized transactions, or fraudulent activities. Early detection allows individuals to take corrective action and safeguard their financial assets.
4. Tax Compliance: Keeping accurate records of financial transactions simplifies tax preparation and ensures compliance with tax regulations. Individuals can easily access the information needed to report income, deductions, and credits accurately.

Examples and Case Studies:

1. The Case of Overspending:

Scenario: Sarah notices that she consistently exceeds her budget for dining out each month. By tracking her transactions, she realizes that she often orders takeout impulsively without considering the cumulative cost. Sarah adjusts her spending habits and allocates more funds to groceries, reducing her dining expenses significantly.

2. Detecting Fraudulent Activity:

Scenario: John receives his credit card statement and notices several unauthorized transactions. He immediately contacts his bank to report the suspicious activity and freezes his card. Thanks to his vigilance in tracking transactions, John prevents further fraudulent charges and avoids financial losses.

3. Tax Preparation Made Easy:

Scenario: Emily keeps meticulous records of her income, expenses, and investment transactions throughout the year. When tax season arrives, she quickly generates reports from her financial tracking software and provides the necessary documentation to her tax preparer. As a result, Emily files her taxes accurately and receives a timely refund. Tools and Strategies:

1. Personal Finance Software: Utilize personal finance software such as Mint, YNAB (You Need A Budget) to track transactions, categorize expenses, and generate reports. These tools offer features like budgeting, bill reminders, and investment tracking to help individuals stay organized.
2. Mobile Banking Apps: Many banks offer mobile banking apps that allow customers to view account balances, monitor transactions, and set up alerts for suspicious activity. These apps provide convenient access to financial information on the go.

3. Spreadsheets: For individuals who prefer a more hands-on approach, creating a simple spreadsheet in Excel or Google Sheets can be an effective way to track transactions and expenses. Customize the spreadsheet to suit your specific needs and update it regularly.
4. Receipt Tracking: Save receipts for all purchases and enter them into your tracking system promptly. This practice ensures that every transaction is accounted for and helps reconcile statements accurately.

Conclusion:

Keeping track of financial transactions and statements is a fundamental aspect of personal financial management. It empowers individuals to make informed decisions, detect errors and fraud, comply with tax regulations, and achieve financial goals. By leveraging tools and strategies and developing a habit of regular monitoring, individuals can maintain financial health and build a solid foundation for future success.

CHAPTER 13

L. LEVERAGING TAX-SAVING STRATEGIES TO OPTIMIZE RETURNS

Introduction:

Understanding and implementing tax-saving strategies is essential for maximizing returns on investments and preserving wealth. In this chapter, weâll explore the importance of leveraging tax-saving strategies, provide practical examples, anecdotes, and discuss effective methods to optimize returns while minimizing tax liabilities.

The Significance of Tax-Saving Strategies:

1. Maximizing Returns: Tax-saving strategies enable individuals to retain more of their income and

investment gains, thereby increasing overall returns on investments.

2. Preserving Wealth: By minimizing tax liabilities, individuals can preserve and grow their wealth over time, ensuring financial security and stability for themselves and their families.

3. Enhancing Cash Flow: Implementing tax-saving strategies can improve cash flow by reducing tax obligations, allowing individuals to allocate more funds towards savings, investments, or other financial goals.

4. Compliance and Efficiency: Understanding and utilizing tax-saving strategies ensure compliance with tax laws and regulations while optimizing financial efficiency and effectiveness.

Examples and Anecdotes:

1. The Retirement Investor:

Scenario: Mark, a diligent saver, contributes regularly to his retirement accounts. By taking advantage of tax-deferred contributions, Mark reduces his taxable income each year, thereby lowering his current tax bill and maximizing his retirement savings. As a result, Mark enjoys significant tax savings over the long term and is well-positioned for a comfortable retirement.

L. Leveraging Tax-Saving Strategies to Optimize Returns

2. The Small Business Owner:

Scenario: Sarah, a small business owner, leverages various tax-saving strategies to optimize her tax position. She takes advantage of business deductions for expenses such as office supplies, equipment, and business travel. Additionally, Sarah structures her business as a small Corporation to minimize self-employment taxes and maximizes retirement contributions. These strategies help Sarah reduce her tax burden and reinvest more of her earnings back into her business.

3. The Real Estate Investor:

Scenario: Emily invests in real estate properties as part of her investment portfolio. She utilizes tax-saving strategies specific to real estate, such as depreciation deductions, to minimize taxes on rental income and capital gains. By strategically managing her real estate investments, Emily generates substantial tax savings while building wealth through property appreciation and rental income.

Effective Tax-Saving Strategies:

1. Retirement Contributions: Contribute to tax-advantaged retirement accounts to reduce taxable income and defer taxes on investment gains until retirement.

2. Tax-Deferred Investments: Invest in tax-deferred vehicles such as annuities, municipal bonds, or certain life insurance policies to defer taxes on investment earnings until withdrawal.
3. Capital Gains Management: Utilize tax-loss harvesting to offset capital gains with capital losses, thereby reducing overall tax liabilities on investment gains.
4. Charitable Giving: Take advantage of tax deductions for charitable donations by contributing to qualified charities or establishing donor-advised funds.

Conclusion:

Leveraging tax-saving strategies is essential for optimizing returns on investments and preserving wealth over the long term. By understanding the significance of tax efficiency and implementing effective strategies such as retirement contributions, tax-deferred investments, capital gains management, and charitable giving, individuals can minimize tax liabilities, maximize returns, and achieve their financial goals with greater efficiency and effectiveness.

CHAPTER 14

M. MINIMIZE UNNECESSARY EXPENSES TO MAXIMIZE SAVINGS

*I*n the pursuit of financial stability and security, one of the fundamental principles is to minimize unnecessary expenses. By doing so, you can effectively maximize your savings, allowing you to build wealth, achieve your financial goals, and secure a comfortable future for yourself and your loved ones.

Understanding Unnecessary Expenses

Unnecessary expenses are those expenditures that bring little to no long-term value or satisfaction to your life. They are often impulse purchases, frivolous indulgences, or recurring costs that could be reduced or eliminated without significantly impacting your quality of life.

Examples of Unnecessary Expenses:

1. Daily Coffee Shop Visits: Consider the habitual morning coffee run. While indulging in a latte or cappuccino might provide a temporary boost, the cumulative cost over time can be staggering. Brewing your coffee at home or in the office can save hundreds or even thousands of dollars annually.
2. Subscription Overload: With the rise of subscription services for entertainment, streaming, fitness, and more, it is easy to accumulate a slew of subscriptions that go underutilized. Assess which subscriptions truly add value to your life and cancel the rest.
3. Impulse Buys: Whether it is clothing, gadgets, or home decor, impulse purchases can quickly derail your budget. Before making a non-essential purchase, ask yourself if it aligns with your long-term financial goals and if you truly need it.

Anecdotes of Successful Expense Minimization

The Lunch-Packing Enthusiast: Sarah, a diligent saver, used to buy lunch from expensive downtown cafes every workday. Realizing the drain on her finances, she began meal prepping on Sundays, packing her lunches for the week. Not only did she save hundreds of dollars each month, but she also enjoyed healthier, homemade meals.

M. Minimize Unnecessary Expenses to Maximize Savings

The Subscription Audit: Mark, a tech enthusiast, found himself subscribed to multiple streaming services, gaming platforms, and magazine subscriptions. Upon realizing he rarely used most of them, he conducted a thorough audit, canceling redundant and underutilized subscriptions. This simple act saved him over $500 annually.

The DIY Home Decor Maven: Emily had a knack for home decor and would often find herself splurging on trendy accent pieces for her apartment. However, after assessing her expenses, she decided to channel her creativity into DIY projects instead. Not only did she save money, but she also discovered a fulfilling hobby and gained a sense of accomplishment from decorating her space with handmade items.

Implementing Expense Minimization Strategies

1. Budget Analysis: Regularly review your expenses to identify areas where you can cut back. Look for recurring expenses that no longer align with your priorities or bring you joy.
2. Differentiate Between Needs and Wants: Before making a purchase, pause and evaluate whether itâs a necessity or a luxury. This simple mindfulness exercise can prevent impulse spending.
3. Automate Savings: Set up automatic transfers from your checking account to your savings or investment

accounts. By prioritizing savings before spending, you will adjust your lifestyle to live within your means.

Conclusion

Minimizing unnecessary expenses is a cornerstone of financial prudence. By consciously evaluating your spending habits, making strategic cuts, and redirecting those funds towards savings and investments, you can achieve greater financial freedom and security. Remember, it is not about depriving yourself of life's pleasures but rather prioritizing your long-term financial well-being.

CHAPTER 15

N. NURTURE A MINDSET OF FRUGALITY AND RESOURCEFULNESS

In the journey towards financial independence and success, cultivating a mindset of frugality and resourcefulness can be a powerful asset. This chapter delves into the importance of embracing frugality and resourcefulness, providing examples and anecdotes to illustrate their impact on personal finances and overall well-being.

Understanding Frugality and Resourcefulness

Frugality is the practice of being economical with resources, avoiding waste, and prioritizing value in spending. Resourcefulness, on the other hand, is the ability to find creative solutions to problems and make the most out of limited resources.

Together, they form a mindset that encourages prudent decision-making and innovative problem-solving.

Examples of Frugality and Resourcefulness:

1. DIY Home Repairs: Instead of immediately hiring a professional for every home repair task, frugal individuals often opt to learn how to fix minor issues themselves. Whether it is fixing a leaky faucet, patching up drywall, or painting a room, DIY approaches can save significant amounts of money over time.
2. Meal Planning and Cooking: Embracing frugality involves cooking meals at home instead of dining out frequently. Resourceful individuals take this a step further by planning meals around ingredients that are on sale or in-season, maximizing savings without sacrificing taste or nutrition.
3. Second-Hand Shopping: Rather than buying brand-new items at retail prices, frugal individuals scour thrift stores, online marketplaces, and garage sales for gently used goods. Resourcefulness comes into play when they repurpose or refurbish these items to fit their needs, saving money while reducing waste.

Anecdotes of Frugality and Resourcefulness

The Budget Wedding Savers: Lisa and Tom wanted to have a memorable wedding without breaking the bank. Instead of splurging on expensive venues and vendors, they embraced frugality by hosting their ceremony and reception in a family member's backyard. Through resourcefulness, they enlisted the help of friends and family for decorations, catering, and entertainment, creating a personalized and budget-friendly celebration.

The Minimalist Nomads: Sarah and Mark decided to downsize their belongings and embrace a minimalist lifestyle. By selling or donating items they no longer needed, they not only decluttered their living space but also generated extra cash. Through frugality, they found creative ways to repurpose existing possessions and live comfortably with less.

The DIY Enthusiasts: James and Emily were passionate about home improvement but had limited funds for renovations. Instead of hiring contractors, they watched online tutorials, borrowed tools from friends, and tackled projects themselves. Through trial and error, they transformed their fixer-upper into a cozy and inviting home, all while staying within their budget.

Implementing Frugality and Resourcefulness Strategies

1. Prioritize Needs Over Wants: Practice discernment when making purchasing decisions, focusing on necessities rather than indulgences.

2. Embrace Minimalism: Simplify your life by decluttering possessions, reducing materialistic desires, and prioritizing experiences over material goods.
3. Invest in Skills and Knowledge: Instead of relying solely on paid services, invest time and effort into learning new skills that empower you to tackle tasks independently.

Conclusion

Nurturing a mindset of frugality and resourcefulness is not just about saving money as it is about embracing a lifestyle that prioritizes efficiency, sustainability, and self-reliance. By adopting frugal habits, practicing resourcefulness, and finding satisfaction in simplicity, you can achieve financial freedom, reduce stress, and live a more fulfilling life. Remember, it is not about deprivation, but rather about making intentional choices that align with your values and long-term goals.

CHAPTER 16

O. OPTIMIZE SPENDING BY PRIORITIZING NEEDS OVER WANTS

*I*n the realm of personal finance, one of the most effective strategies for achieving financial stability and freedom is to optimize spending by prioritizing needs over wants. This chapter explores the importance of distinguishing between needs and wants, providing examples and anecdotes to illustrate how prioritizing needs can lead to more prudent financial decisions.

Understanding Needs vs. Wants

Needs are essential for survival and well-being, encompassing fundamental necessities such as food, shelter, clothing, healthcare, and transportation. Wants, on the other hand, are desires that enhance comfort, convenience, or enjoyment but are not strictly necessary for survival. By prioritizing needs over wants, individuals can allocate their resources more effectively, ensuring that essential expenses are covered before indulging in discretionary purchases.

Examples of Needs vs. Wants:

1. Housing: Rent or mortgage payments for a modest, functional dwelling fulfill the need for shelter. Upgrading to a larger, more luxurious home with additional amenities may satisfy wants but can strain finances unnecessarily.
2. Transportation: Owning a reliable vehicle for commuting to work or fulfilling family obligations addresses the need for transportation. Opting for a luxury car or frequent vehicle upgrades may be desirable but can lead to inflated expenses that exceed transportation needs.
3. Food: Purchasing nutritious groceries to sustain health and energy fulfills the need for nourishment. Dining out at restaurants or indulging in gourmet foods may provide enjoyment but can quickly inflate food expenses beyond basic nutritional requirements.

Anecdotes of Prioritizing Needs Over Wants

The Practical Homebuyer: Michael, a first-time homebuyer, prioritized his needs when searching for a residence. Instead of fixating on extravagant features or trendy neighborhoods, he focused on finding a modest home within his budget that met his family's essential needs. By prioritizing affordability and functionality, he avoided becoming house poor and maintained financial flexibility.

The Budget-Conscious Traveler: Sarah, an avid traveler, embraced the philosophy of prioritizing needs over wants when planning her vacations. Instead of splurging on luxury accommodations and extravagant excursions, she opted for budget-friendly accommodations and sought out free or low-cost attractions. By prioritizing experiences over lavish accommodations, she was able to travel more frequently without straining her finances.

The Minimalist Lifestyle Advocate: David, inspired by the minimalist movement, made a conscious effort to prioritize needs over wants in his daily life. He decluttered his living space, sold unnecessary possessions, and limited discretionary spending to essentials. By adopting a minimalist mindset and focusing on simplicity and functionality, he achieved greater financial freedom and peace of mind.

Implementing Prioritization Strategies

1. Create a Budget: Allocate a portion of your income to cover essential needs such as housing, utilities, food, healthcare, and transportation before allocating funds to discretionary spending categories.

2. Practice Delayed Gratification: Before making a non-essential purchase, pause and consider whether it aligns with your long-term financial goals and priorities. Delaying gratification can help distinguish between genuine needs and fleeting wants.
3. Evaluate Value Propositions: When considering purchases, assess the value proposition by weighing the benefits and drawbacks of each expenditure. Focus on investments that provide long-term utility and satisfaction rather than short-term gratification.

Conclusion

Optimizing spending by prioritizing needs over wants is a foundational principle of prudent financial management. By distinguishing between essential expenses and discretionary indulgences, individuals can allocate their resources more effectively, achieve greater financial stability, and pursue their long-term goals with confidence. Remember, it is not about deprivation but rather about making intentional choices that align with your values and priorities.

CHAPTER 17

P. PLAN FOR RETIREMENT AND CREATE A SUSTAINABLE INCOME STREAM

Retirement planning is a critical aspect of financial well-being, ensuring that individuals can maintain their desired lifestyle and enjoy financial security during their golden years. This chapter explores the importance of retirement planning and provides examples and anecdotes to illustrate strategies for creating a sustainable income stream in retirement.

The Significance of Retirement Planning

Retirement represents a significant life transition where individuals transition from relying on earned income to living off accumulated savings and investments.

Planning for retirement allows individuals to build a financial safety net, mitigate risks, and enjoy a comfortable lifestyle without financial stress.

Why Retirement Planning Matters:

1. Financial Security: Planning for retirement enables individuals to accumulate sufficient funds to cover living expenses, healthcare costs, and leisure activities during retirement.
2. Longevity Risk: With increasing life expectancy, individuals may spend decades in retirement, requiring adequate savings to sustain their lifestyle over the long term.
3. Inflation and Market Volatility: Retirement planning involves accounting for inflation and market fluctuations, ensuring that savings and investments can withstand economic challenges.

Anecdotes of Retirement Planning Success

The Early Retirement Enthusiasts: John and Lisa dreamed of retiring early to pursue their passions and travel the world. They diligently saved a significant portion of their income, maxed out their retirement accounts, and invested in diversified portfolios.

Through disciplined saving and investing, they achieved financial independence in their early 40s, allowing them to retire comfortably and enjoy a fulfilling lifestyle.

The Retirement Income Strategist: Sarah, nearing retirement age, devised a comprehensive income strategy to sustain her lifestyle in retirement. She diversified her income sources, including Social Security benefits, pension payments, rental income from investment properties, and dividends from a balanced investment portfolio. By creating multiple streams of income, she ensured financial stability and flexibility in retirement. By planning my own retirement a decade ahead, now we have multiple streams of income and are financially secure.

The Late Bloomer: Mark, a late bloomer in retirement planning, realized the importance of saving for retirement in his 50s. Despite starting relatively late, he prioritized aggressive savings and investment strategies, including maximizing contributions to retirement accounts and investing in high-yield assets. Through disciplined saving and prudent investment decisions, he successfully built a sizable nest egg, allowing him to retire comfortably on his own terms.

Strategies for Creating a Sustainable Income Stream

1. Start Early: Begin saving for retirement as early as possible to leverage the power of compounding and accumulate wealth over time.
2. Maximize Retirement Accounts: Take advantage of employer-sponsored retirement plans like NPS or National Pension Savings scheme or individual retirement accounts (IRAs) to maximize tax-advantaged savings opportunities.
3. Diversify Investments: Build a diversified investment portfolio consisting of stocks, bonds, real estate, and other asset classes to mitigate risk and optimize returns.
4. Consider Annuities and Social Security: Explore options such as annuities and Social Security benefits to create guaranteed income streams that provide financial stability in retirement.
5. Plan for Healthcare Costs: Factor in healthcare expenses when planning for retirement, including Medicare premiums, supplemental insurance, and potential long-term care needs.

Conclusion

Planning for retirement and creating a sustainable income stream are essential steps towards achieving financial security and peace of mind in later years. By starting early, diversifying income sources, and making informed investment decisions, individuals can build a robust financial foundation that supports their desired lifestyle in retirement. Remember, retirement planning is a journey that requires careful consideration and ongoing adjustments to adapt to changing circumstances and priorities.

CHAPTER 18

Q. QUESTION FINANCIAL ADVICE AND SEEK MULTIPLE PERSPECTIVES

*I*n the complex landscape of personal finance, it is essential to approach financial advice with a critical mindset and seek multiple perspectives to make informed decisions. This chapter delves into the importance of questioning financial advice and provides examples and anecdotes to illustrate the benefits of seeking diverse viewpoints.

The Value of Questioning Financial Advice

While seeking guidance from financial experts and advisors can be invaluable, blindly following advice without critical evaluation can lead to suboptimal outcomes.

Questioning financial advice allows individuals to gain deeper insights, identify potential biases or conflicts of interest, and tailor recommendations to their unique circumstances and goals.

Why Questioning Financial Advice Matters:

1. Individualized Solutions: Financial advice should be tailored to individual circumstances, taking into account factors such as risk tolerance, financial goals, and life stage.
2. Mitigating Risks: Questioning financial advice helps identify potential risks and drawbacks, allowing individuals to make informed decisions that align with their risk tolerance and preferences.
3. Avoiding Bias: Financial advisors may have biases or conflicts of interest that influence their recommendations. Questioning advice helps uncover potential biases and ensures that recommendations are objective and impartial.

Anecdotes of Questioning Financial Advice

The Sceptical Investor: David, skeptical of the prevailing investment advice to buy and hold a diversified portfolio of index funds, conducted extensive research and sought multiple perspectives. After critically evaluating various investment strategies, he opted for a hybrid approach that combined passive index investing with active stock selection based on fundamental analysis. By questioning conventional wisdom and seeking alternative viewpoints, David achieved superior investment returns tailored to his risk tolerance and investment objectives.

The Inquisitive Entrepreneur: Sarah, an aspiring entrepreneur, sought advice from seasoned business owners and industry experts before launching her startup.

Instead of blindly following conventional startup advice, she questioned assumptions, challenged conventional wisdom, and solicited diverse perspectives. Through rigorous questioning and critical thinking, Sarah developed a business model that addressed market needs, mitigated risks, and maximized growth potential, leading to a successful launch and sustainable growth.

The Discerning Consumer: Mark, in the market for financial products such as insurance policies and investment funds, diligently researched options and solicited recommendations from multiple sources. Instead of relying solely on recommendations from financial advisors or sales representatives, he sought input from trusted friends, family members, and online communities. By questioning financial advice and seeking diverse perspectives, Mark identified products that aligned with his needs, preferences, and risk tolerance, avoiding costly mistakes and achieving optimal outcomes.

Strategies for Questioning Financial Advice

1. Do Your Own Research: Conduct independent research to understand financial concepts, products, and strategies before seeking advice from professionals.
2. Seek Diverse Perspectives: Consult multiple sources, including financial advisors, experts, peers, and online resources, to gain a comprehensive understanding of different viewpoints and approaches.
3. Ask Critical Questions: Challenge assumptions, explore potential risks and drawbacks, and seek clarification on ambiguous or conflicting advice to make informed decisions.
4. Consider the Source: Evaluate the credentials, expertise, and potential biases of individuals offering financial advice to assess the credibility and relevance of their recommendations.

Conclusion

Questioning financial advice and seeking multiple perspectives are essential practices for making informed decisions and achieving financial success. By adopting a critical mindset, conducting independent research, and soliciting diverse viewpoints, individuals can tailor financial strategies to their unique circumstances, preferences, and goals. Remember, financial advice is not one-size-fits-all, and the best approach is often a product of thoughtful analysis, careful consideration, and openness to alternative viewpoints.

CHAPTER 19

R. RESEARCH AND UNDERSTAND INVESTMENT OPPORTUNITIES BEFORE COMMITTING

*I*nvesting is a crucial component of building wealth and achieving financial goals, but it comes with inherent risks. This chapter explores the importance of thorough research and understanding investment opportunities before committing capital, with examples and anecdotes highlighting the benefits of informed decision-making.

The Importance of Research in Investing

Investing involves allocating capital to assets with the expectation of generating returns. However, not all investment opportunities are created equal, and thorough research is essential to assess risks, evaluate potential

R. Research and Understand Investment Opportunities Before Committing

returns, and make informed decisions that align with financial objectives.

Why Researching Investments Matters:

1. Risk Mitigation: Researching investments helps identify risks and potential pitfalls, allowing investors to make informed decisions and mitigate the probability of losses.
2. Return Maximization: Understanding investment opportunities enables investors to identify assets with strong growth potential and attractive risk-adjusted returns, maximizing the potential for wealth accumulation.
3. Alignment with Goals: Researching investments ensures that capital is allocated to assets that align with financial goals, risk tolerance, and investment time horizon, optimizing portfolio performance and achieving desired outcomes.

Anecdotes of Researching Investments

The Diligent Stock Investor: Sarah, an aspiring stock investor, spent months researching individual companies before making her first investment. She analyzed financial statements, researched industry trends, and evaluated competitive positioning to identify undervalued stocks with growth potential. Through diligent research and patience, Sarah built a diversified portfolio of high-quality companies and achieved significant returns over time.

The Thorough Real Estate Investor: Mark, interested in real estate investing, conducted extensive research before purchasing his first rental property. He analyzed local market trends, assessed rental demand, and performed thorough due diligence on prospective properties. By meticulously researching investment opportunities and understanding the dynamics of the real estate market, Mark acquired properties with strong cash flow potential and achieved consistent rental income.

The Informed Cryptocurrency Investor: David, intrigued by the potential of cryptocurrencies, delved into the intricacies of blockchain technology and the fundamentals of various digital assets. He researched whitepapers, studied project teams, and analyzed market dynamics to identify promising cryptocurrencies with long-term viability. Through diligent research and a deep understanding of the cryptocurrency landscape, David navigated volatile markets and capitalized on lucrative investment opportunities.

Strategies for Researching Investments

1. Understand the Asset Class: Gain a thorough understanding of the characteristics, risks, and potential returns associated with different asset classes,

such as stocks, bonds, real estate, and alternative investments.

2. Conduct Due Diligence: Perform comprehensive due diligence on investment opportunities, including analyzing financial data, researching market trends, and assessing competitive positioning.
3. Seek Expert Advice: Consult financial advisors, industry experts, and experienced investors for insights and perspectives on investment opportunities, leveraging their expertise to inform decision-making.
4. Stay Informed: Stay abreast of market developments, regulatory changes, and macroeconomic trends that may impact investment performance, continually updating research and analysis to adapt to evolving conditions.

Conclusion

Researching and understanding investment opportunities before committing capital is essential for success in the financial markets. By conducting thorough due diligence, analyzing risks and potential returns, and aligning investments with financial goals and risk tolerance, investors can make informed decisions that maximize the likelihood of achieving desired outcomes. Remember, investing is a journey that requires continuous learning, adaptation, and disciplined decision- making to navigate opportunities and challenges effectively.

CHAPTER 20

S. SET ACHIEVABLE FINANCIAL GOALS AND MILESTONES

*S*etting achievable financial goals and milestones is the cornerstone of a successful financial plan. This chapter explores the importance of goal setting, providing examples and anecdotes to illustrate how it can lead to greater financial stability, motivation, and success.

The Significance of Setting Financial Goals

Financial goals serve as guideposts that direct individuals towards their desired financial future. Whether it is saving for a down payment on a home, funding a child's education, or building a retirement nest egg, setting clear and achievable financial goals provides focus, motivation, and a roadmap for success.

S. Set Achievable Financial Goals and Milestones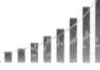

Why Setting Financial Goals Matters:

1. Clarity and Focus: Setting financial goals clarifies priorities and motivates individuals to take concrete steps towards achieving them, fostering discipline and determination.
2. Measurement and Progress Tracking: Establishing specific, measurable goals allows individuals to track their progress over time, celebrate milestones, and make adjustments as needed to stay on course.
3. Long-Term Planning: Setting long-term financial goals helps individuals envision their desired lifestyle in the future, enabling them to make informed decisions and allocate resources effectively to achieve those goals.

Anecdotes of Setting Financial Goals

The Homeownership Dreamer: Sarah, a young professional, dreamed of owning her own home. She set a specific financial goal to save for a down payment within five years. To achieve this goal, she created a detailed budget, automated savings contributions, and tracked her progress diligently. Despite facing challenges and temptations along the way, Sarah remained focused on her goal and successfully purchased her dream home within the specified timeframe.

The Debt-Free Achiever: Mark, burdened by student loan debt, set a goal to become debt-free within ten years. He developed a repayment plan that prioritized high-interest loans and allocated extra funds towards debt reduction each month.

Through discipline, sacrifice, and determination, Mark paid off his student loans ahead of schedule, achieving financial freedom and setting the stage for future financial success.

The Early Retirement Planner: David, inspired by the concept of financial independence, set a goal to retire early and pursue his passions. He calculated the amount of savings required to sustain his desired lifestyle in retirement and devised a savings plan that aligned with his goal. Through diligent saving, investing, and lifestyle adjustments, David achieved his goal of early retirement, enjoying a fulfilling life free from financial constraints.

Strategies for Setting Financial Goals

1. Be Specific and Realistic: Set clear, measurable financial goals that are achievable within a reasonable timeframe, considering factors such as income, expenses, and current financial circumstances.
2. Prioritize Goals: Rank financial goals based on importance and urgency, focusing on high-priority goals while maintaining flexibility to adjust as circumstances change.

3. Break Down Goals into Milestones: Divide long-term goals into smaller, achievable milestones, allowing for incremental progress and maintaining motivation throughout the journey.
4. Regularly Review and Adjust: Periodically review financial goals and milestones, reassessing priorities, progress, and timelines, and making adjustments as needed to stay on track.

Conclusion

Setting achievable financial goals and milestones is essential for achieving financial success and realizing dreams. By establishing clear objectives, staying focused, and taking consistent action, individuals can overcome obstacles, stay motivated, and make meaningful progress towards their financial aspirations. Remember, the journey to financial success is not linear, and it requires patience, perseverance, and adaptability to navigate challenges and seize opportunities along the way.

CHAPTER 21

T. TAKE CALCULATED RISKS FOR POTENTIAL FINANCIAL GROWTH

*T*aking calculated risks is an essential aspect of financial growth and wealth accumulation. In this chapter, we explore the significance of embracing calculated risks, providing examples and anecdotes to illustrate how prudent risk-taking can lead to significant financial rewards.

Understanding Calculated Risks

Calculated risks involve carefully evaluating potential opportunities and weighing the potential rewards against the associated risks. While all investments carry some level of risk, taking calculated risks involves conducting thorough due diligence, managing risk exposure, and making informed decisions that align with financial goals and risk tolerance.

Why Taking Calculated Risks Matters:

1. Potential for Growth: Embracing calculated risks opens up opportunities for financial growth and wealth accumulation beyond what is achievable through conservative strategies alone.
2. Innovation and Progress: Taking calculated risks fosters innovation, creativity, and entrepreneurship, driving economic growth and societal progress.
3. Learning and Adaptation: Even if a calculated risk does not yield the desired outcome, the experience provides valuable lessons and insights that can inform future decision-making and improve risk management capabilities.

Anecdotes of Taking Calculated Risks

The Entrepreneurial Visionary: Sarah, with a bold vision for a tech startup, took a calculated risk by quitting her stable job to pursue entrepreneurship full-time. She conducted market research, developed a viable business plan, and secured initial funding from investors. Despite facing challenges and setbacks along the way, Sarah's calculated risk paid off as her startup gained traction, attracted customers, and eventually became a successful venture, generating substantial financial returns.

The Strategic Investor: Mark, intrigued by the potential of emerging markets, took a calculated risk by allocating a portion of his investment portfolio to high-growth stocks in developing economies. He conducted thorough research, diversified his investments, and monitored market trends closely. While the investments were inherently risky due to geopolitical uncertainties and market volatility, Mark's calculated risk paid off handsomely as his portfolio outperformed expectations, delivering significant financial growth over time.

The Property Investor: David, recognizing the potential of real estate investment, took a calculated risk by purchasing an investment property in a burgeoning neighborhood. He conducted due diligence, analyzed rental demand, and assessed potential returns. Despite initial apprehension and uncertainty, David's calculated risk paid off as the property appreciated in value, generated rental income, and provided a steady stream of cash flow, contributing to his overall financial growth and stability.

Strategies for Taking Calculated Risks

1. Conduct Thorough Due Diligence: Research potential opportunities extensively, gathering relevant data, analyzing market trends, and assessing potential risks and rewards before making investment decisions.
2. Manage Risk Exposure: Diversify investments across different asset classes, industries, and geographic regions to spread risk and minimize exposure to any single risk factor.

3. Stay Informed and Adaptive: Stay abreast of market developments, regulatory changes, and emerging trends, adapting investment strategies and risk management approaches accordingly to capitalize on opportunities and mitigate risks.
4. Maintain a Long-Term Perspective: Take a long-term view when assessing potential risks and rewards, focusing on fundamental value drivers and avoiding short-term speculation or impulse decisions.

Conclusion

Taking calculated risks is an essential component of achieving financial growth and wealth accumulation. By carefully evaluating opportunities, managing risk exposure, and making informed decisions that align with financial goals and risk tolerance, individuals can unlock new avenues for growth and capitalize on opportunities that lead to significant financial rewards. Remember, while calculated risks involve uncertainty, they also present opportunities for innovation, learning, and progress that can propel individuals towards their financial aspirations and goals.

CHAPTER 22

U. UTILIZE BUDGETING TOOLS AND TECHNIQUES EFFECTIVELY

*B*udgeting is the foundation of financial management, providing a roadmap for achieving financial goals and maintaining control over spending. In this chapter, we explore the importance of utilizing budgeting tools and techniques effectively, offering examples, anecdotes, and practical strategies for mastering the art of budgeting.

The Significance of Budgeting Tools and Techniques

Budgeting tools and techniques empower individuals to track income, expenses, and savings, enabling them to make informed financial decisions and achieve financial stability. By utilizing budgeting tools effectively, individuals can gain clarity and control over their finances, identify areas for improvement, and work towards their financial goals with confidence.

Why Utilizing Budgeting Tools Matters:

1. Financial Awareness: Budgeting tools provide insights into income, expenses, and savings, enhancing financial awareness and fostering responsible money management habits.
2. Goal Alignment: By tracking spending and saving patterns, individuals can ensure that their financial decisions align with their long-term goals and priorities.
3. Decision Support: Budgeting tools offer data-driven insights and analysis, empowering individuals to make informed decisions about spending, saving, and investing to optimize financial outcomes.

Anecdotes of Effective Budgeting Tools and Techniques

The Digital Budgeting Maverick: Sarah, overwhelmed by the complexities of managing her finances, turned to digital budgeting tools for help. She discovered user-friendly apps like Mint and You Need a Budget (YNAB), which offered features such as expense tracking, budget categorization, and goal setting. By leveraging these tools effectively, Sarah gained clarity over her finances, identified areas for savings, and made informed decisions that aligned with her financial goals, ultimately achieving greater financial stability and peace of mind.

The Spreadsheet Savvy Saver: Mark, a spreadsheet enthusiast, created a customized budgeting spreadsheet to track his income, expenses, and savings goals. He meticulously organized his finances, categorizing expenses, and setting budget targets for each category. By regularly updating his spreadsheet and analyzing spending patterns, Mark identified areas for optimization, adjusted his budget accordingly, and made significant progress towards his financial goals, all while maintaining control over his finances.

The Envelope Budgeting Proponent: David, inspired by the envelope budgeting method, implemented a physical envelope system to manage his discretionary spending. He allocated cash to different envelopes for categories such as groceries, dining out, and entertainment, limiting spending to the predetermined amounts in each envelope. By adhering to the envelope system, David maintained discipline in his spending habits, avoided overspending, and achieved greater control over his discretionary expenses, ultimately contributing to his overall financial well-being.

Strategies for Utilizing Budgeting Tools and Techniques Effectively

1. Choose the Right Tools: Explore various budgeting tools and platforms to find one that suits your preferences, needs, and financial goals.

2. Set Realistic Goals: Establish clear, achievable financial goals and use budgeting tools to track progress towards these goals, adjusting as needed to stay on track.
3. Stay Consistent: Make budgeting a habit by consistently tracking income, expenses, and savings, ensuring that financial decisions are informed by accurate and up-to-date data.
4. Review and Adjust Regularly: Periodically review your budget, analyze spending patterns, and adjust allocations as needed to optimize financial outcomes and adapt to changing circumstances.

Conclusion

Utilizing budgeting tools and techniques effectively is essential for achieving financial stability, managing spending, and working towards financial goals. Whether through digital apps, spreadsheets, or traditional methods like envelope budgeting, individuals can gain clarity, control, and confidence over their finances by implementing effective budgeting strategies. Remember, budgeting is not a one- size-fits-all approach, and it may require experimentation, adaptation, and continuous improvement to find a method that works best for your unique financial circumstances and goals.

CHAPTER 23

V. VALUE LONG-TERM FINANCIAL STABILITY OVER SHORT-TERM GAINS

*I*n the fast-paced world of finance, it is easy to get caught up in the allure of short-term gains. However, prioritizing long-term financial stability over short-term gains is essential for building lasting wealth and security. This chapter explores the importance of valuing long-term stability, offering examples, anecdotes, and practical strategies for achieving financial success over time.

The Importance of Long-Term Financial Stability

Long-term financial stability provides a foundation for peace of mind, enabling individuals to weather economic downturns, unexpected expenses, and life transitions with confidence. By prioritizing long-term stability over short-term gains, individuals can build sustainable wealth, achieve financial independence, and secure their future for years to come.

Why Valuing Long-Term Stability Matters:

1. Resilience in Adversity: Long-term financial stability provides a buffer against unforeseen challenges, enabling individuals to navigate financial hardships and emergencies without jeopardizing their financial well-being.
2. Wealth Accumulation: By focusing on long-term growth rather than short- term fluctuations, individuals can accumulate wealth steadily over time through strategic saving, investing, and prudent financial management.
3. Peace of Mind: Prioritizing long-term stability fosters a sense of security and confidence, allowing individuals to focus on their goals, aspirations, and well-being without constantly worrying about financial instability or uncertainty.

Anecdotes of Valuing Long-Term Financial Stability

The Patient Investor: Sarah, an investor with a long-term mindset, resisted the temptation to chase short-term market trends and instead focused on building a diversified portfolio of high-quality assets. Despite experiencing market volatility and fluctuations, Sarah remained disciplined in her investment approach, staying committed to her long-term financial goals. Over time, her patience and perseverance paid off as her investments grew steadily, providing a reliable source of income and wealth accumulation.

The Frugal Saver: Mark, a frugal individual with a focus on long-term stability, prioritized saving and investing for the future over indulging in immediate gratification. Despite facing pressure from peers and societal norms to spend lavishly, Mark maintained a modest lifestyle, prioritizing savings, and investments in assets with long-term growth potential. As a result, he built a sizable nest egg over time, achieving financial independence and security for himself and his family.

The Strategic Planner: David, a strategic planner with a long-term perspective, carefully mapped out his financial goals and devised a comprehensive plan to achieve them over time. He diversified his income sources, prioritized debt repayment, and invested in assets with long-term growth potential. Through disciplined saving, investing, and prudent financial management, David steadily progressed towards his long-term goals, ultimately achieving financial stability and peace of mind.

Strategies for Valuing Long-Term Financial Stability

1. Define Clear Goals: Establish clear, achievable financial goals that align with long-term stability, such as building an emergency fund, saving for retirement, or paying off debt.
2. Develop a Strategic Plan: Create a comprehensive financial plan that outlines steps for achieving long-term stability, including saving, investing, debt management, and risk mitigation strategies.
3. Practice Patience and Discipline: Stay committed to your long-term financial goals, even in the face of short-term challenges or temptations, exercising patience and discipline in your financial decisions.
4. Focus on Fundamentals: Prioritize fundamental financial principles such as living within your means, saving consistently, and investing prudently to achieve long-term stability and success.

Conclusion

Valuing long-term financial stability over short-term gains is essential for building lasting wealth, security, and peace of mind. By prioritizing strategic planning, disciplined saving, prudent investing, and patience, individuals can achieve their long-term financial goals and secure their future for years to come. Remember, financial success is a journey, not a destination, and it requires consistent effort, commitment, and a focus on the bigger picture to achieve lasting stability and prosperity.

CHAPTER 24

W. WORK TOWARDS BUILDING MULTIPLE STREAMS OF INCOME

*D*iversifying income sources is a key strategy for achieving financial stability and independence. This chapter explores the importance of building multiple streams of income, offering examples, anecdotes, and practical strategies for diversifying income and increasing financial resilience.

The Significance of Multiple Streams of Income

Relying solely on a single source of income can leave individuals vulnerable to financial instability in the face of job loss, economic downturns, or unexpected expenses. Building multiple streams of income provides a safety net, enabling individuals to generate revenue from various sources and mitigate risks associated with dependence on a single income source.

Why Building Multiple Streams of Income Matters:

1. Risk Mitigation: Diversifying income sources spreads risk and reduces dependence on any single source of income, providing financial resilience and stability.
2. Income Growth: Multiple streams of income offer opportunities for increased earning potential and financial growth, allowing individuals to maximize revenue and achieve their financial goals more quickly.
3. Flexibility and Freedom: Diversified income streams provide flexibility and freedom, enabling individuals to pursue diverse interests, passions, and opportunities without relying solely on a traditional job or career path. Anecdotes of Building Multiple Streams of Income

The Side Hustle Entrepreneur: Sarah, a full-time employee with a passion for photography, started a side hustle offering photography services for events and portraits on weekends. By leveraging her skills and interests outside of her primary job, Sarah generated additional income from her photography business, diversifying her revenue streams and increasing her financial resilience. Over time, her side hustle grew into a profitable business, providing a

W. Work Towards Building Multiple Streams of Income

significant source of supplementary income and opening up new opportunities for growth and fulfillment.

The Passive Income Investor: Mark, interested in real estate investing, purchased a rental property and began earning passive income from rental payments.

Encouraged by the success of his first investment, Mark continued to acquire additional rental properties over time, building a portfolio of income-generating assets that provided a steady stream of passive income. By diversifying his income streams through real estate investing, Mark achieved financial independence and security, freeing himself from reliance on a traditional job for income.

The Freelance Gig Worker: David, a skilled graphic designer, supplemented his full- time job by taking on freelance projects in his spare time. By leveraging his expertise and networks in the freelance market, David was able to generate additional income from freelance gigs, diversifying his income streams and increasing his earning potential. Despite the demands of juggling multiple projects, David found fulfillment in his freelance work and enjoyed the financial stability and flexibility it provided.

Strategies for Building Multiple Streams of Income

1. Identify Skills and Interests: Identify skills, talents, and passions that can be monetized to generate additional income, whether through freelance work, consulting, or entrepreneurship.
2. Explore Passive Income Opportunities: Consider investing in income-generating assets such as rental properties, dividend-paying stocks, or royalties from creative work to generate passive income streams.
3. Start Small and Scale Up: Begin by exploring low-risk, low-cost income opportunities and gradually scale up as you gain experience, confidence, and resources.
4. Diversify Income Sources: Build a portfolio of income streams from diverse sources such as employment, self-employment, investments, and passive income sources to spread risk and maximize earning potential.

Conclusion

Building multiple streams of income is a powerful strategy for achieving financial stability, independence, and resilience. By diversifying income sources, individuals can reduce reliance on any single source of income and increase their earning potential, enabling them to achieve their financial goals more quickly and effectively.

Remember, building multiple streams of income takes time, effort, and persistence, but the rewards in terms of financial security, flexibility, and freedom are well worth the investment.

CHAPTER 25

X. X-RAY YOUR FINANCIAL PORTFOLIO FOR WEAKNESSES AND AREAS OF IMPROVEMENT

*C*onducting a thorough examination of your financial portfolio is essential for identifying weaknesses, addressing vulnerabilities, and optimizing performance. In this chapter, we explore the importance of x-raying your financial portfolio, offering examples, anecdotes, and practical strategies for improving financial health and resilience.

The Significance of X-Raying Your Financial Portfolio

Just as a medical x-ray reveals hidden issues within the body, a financial x-ray uncovers weaknesses and vulnerabilities within your financial portfolio. By conducting a comprehensive assessment, individuals can identify areas for improvement, mitigate risks, and optimize their financial strategies for long-term success.

Why X-Raying Your Financial Portfolio Matters:

1. Risk Management: Identifying weaknesses and vulnerabilities allows individuals to mitigate risks and implement strategies to protect against potential threats to financial stability.
2. Optimization: X-raying your financial portfolio reveals opportunities for improvement and optimization, enabling individuals to reallocate resources, streamline expenses, and maximize returns.
3. Long-Term Planning: By assessing the health of your financial portfolio, individuals can develop long-term strategies that align with their goals, aspirations, and risk tolerance, ensuring sustained financial success over time.

Anecdotes of X-Raying Financial Portfolios

The Overleveraged Investor: Sarah, eager to accelerate wealth accumulation, borrowed heavily to invest in high-risk assets with the potential for high returns. However, a thorough x-ray of her financial portfolio revealed that she was overleveraged and exposed to significant risk in the event of market downturns or economic shocks. Sarah adjusted her investment strategy, reducing leverage, diversifying assets, and prioritizing risk management.

By taking proactive steps to address weaknesses in her portfolio, Sarah achieved greater financial resilience and stability.

The Neglected Retirement Account: Mark, focused on day-to-day expenses and short-term financial goals, neglected to review his retirement account regularly. Upon x-raying his financial portfolio, Mark discovered that his retirement savings were not aligned with his long-term objectives, and his investment allocations were suboptimal. Mark rebalanced his retirement portfolio, diversified investments, and increased contributions to align with his retirement goals. By addressing weaknesses in his retirement account, Mark enhanced his prospects for long-term financial security and independence.

The Uninsured Entrepreneur: David, immersed in building his business and pursuing entrepreneurial opportunities, overlooked the importance of insurance coverage to protect against unforeseen risks. After x-raying his financial portfolio, David realized that he was exposed to significant liabilities and lacked adequate insurance protection. He promptly obtained insurance coverage for his business, personal assets, and health, mitigating potential risks and safeguarding his financial well- being. By addressing weaknesses in his insurance coverage, David achieved greater peace of mind and resilience against unexpected events.

Strategies for X-Raying Your Financial Portfolio

1. Review Regularly: Set aside time periodically to review and assess your financial portfolio, including assets, liabilities, income, and expenses.
2. Identify Weaknesses: Analyze your financial portfolio to identify weaknesses, vulnerabilities, and areas for improvement, such as excessive debt, inadequate savings, or suboptimal investment allocations.
3. Take Action: Develop a plan to address weaknesses in your financial portfolio, whether through debt reduction, savings optimization, risk management strategies, or investment reallocation.
4. Seek Professional Advice: Consult with financial advisors, accountants, or other professionals for insights and guidance on optimizing your financial portfolio and addressing specific challenges or concerns.

Conclusion

X- raying your financial portfolio is a crucial step towards achieving financial health, resilience, and success. By identifying weaknesses, vulnerabilities, and areas for improvement, individuals can take proactive steps to mitigate risks, optimize performance, and align their financial strategies with their goals and aspirations.

Remember, financial x-raying is an ongoing process that requires diligence, attention to detail, and a commitment to continuous improvement to ensure long-term financial well-being and prosperity.

CHAPTER 26

Y. YIELD TO PRUDENT FINANCIAL HABITS AND DISCIPLINED MONEY MANAGEMENT

*P*rudent financial habits and disciplined money management are the cornerstones of financial success and stability. In this chapter, we explore the importance of yielding to these principles, offering examples, anecdotes, and practical strategies for cultivating a mindset of responsible financial behavior.

The Significance of Prudent Financial Habits

Prudent financial habits encompass a range of behaviors and practices that promote responsible money management, such as budgeting, saving, investing, and debt management. By adhering to these habits consistently, individuals can achieve financial security, build wealth, and realize their long-term financial goals.

Why Yielding to Prudent Financial Habits Matters:

1. Financial Stability: Prudent financial habits provide a solid foundation for financial stability, enabling individuals to weather economic uncertainties, emergencies, and unexpected expenses with confidence.
2. Wealth Accumulation: Disciplined money management promotes savings, investing, and wealth accumulation over time, allowing individuals to achieve their financial aspirations and build a brighter future for themselves and their families.
3. Peace of Mind: Yielding to prudent financial habits fosters peace of mind and reduces financial stress, empowering individuals to focus on their goals, passions, and well-being without constant worry about money matters.

Anecdotes of Prudent Financial Habits

The Budgeting Maven: Sarah, a meticulous budgeter, diligently tracks her income and expenses using a detailed budgeting spreadsheet. By allocating funds to various categories and monitoring spending closely, Sarah ensures that she lives within her means, avoids overspending, and prioritizes savings and investments. Despite the temptation to indulge in impulse purchases or lifestyle inflation, Sarah's commitment to budgeting allows her to achieve her financial goals and maintain financial stability over the long term.

The Consistent Saver: Mark, a disciplined saver, automates contributions to his savings and investment accounts each month. By paying himself first and treating savings as a non-negotiable expense, Mark ensures that he consistently sets aside a portion of his income for future goals and emergencies. Over time, his consistent saving habits have enabled him to accumulate a substantial nest egg, providing a safety net and opening up opportunities for financial growth and freedom.

The Debt-Free Achiever: David, determined to eliminate debt and achieve financial freedom, adopts a disciplined approach to debt management. He prioritizes debt repayment, allocates extra funds towards paying off loans, and avoids taking on new debt unnecessarily. Despite facing challenges and setbacks along the way, David's commitment to living debt-free allows him to achieve financial independence and pursue his goals with confidence and peace of mind.

Strategies for Prudent Financial Habits and Disciplined Money Management

1. Create a Budget: Develop a budget that outlines income, expenses, savings, and financial goals, and stick to it consistently.
2. Automate Savings: Set up automatic transfers to savings and investment accounts to ensure consistent contributions and avoid the temptation to spend impulsively.
3. Live Below Your Means: Practice frugality and avoid lifestyle inflation by living below your means, prioritizing needs over wants, and resisting the urge to overspend.
4. Pay Yourself First: Treat savings as a non-negotiable expense and prioritize paying yourself first before allocating funds to other expenses or discretionary purchases.

Conclusion

Yielding to prudent financial habits and disciplined money management is essential for achieving financial success, stability, and peace of mind. By adopting responsible behaviors such as budgeting, saving, investing, and debt management, individuals can build a solid financial foundation, realize their long-term goals, and enjoy a brighter financial future. Remember, cultivating these habits requires commitment, discipline, and perseverance, but the rewards in terms of financial security, freedom, and fulfillment are well worth the effort.

CHAPTER 27

Z. ZERO IN ON FINANCIAL INDEPENDENCE AND WEALTH-BUILDING STRATEGIES

*A*chieving financial independence and building wealth are aspirations shared by many. In this chapter, we delve into the importance of zeroing in on these goals, offering examples, anecdotes, and practical strategies for pursuing financial independence and wealth accumulation.

The Significance of Financial Independence and Wealth-Building Strategies

Financial independence represents the ability to live life on your own terms, free from financial constraints or obligations. Wealth-building strategies are the means by which individuals can accumulate assets and resources over time, enabling them to achieve financial independence and pursue their desired lifestyle.

Why Zeroing in on Financial Independence and Wealth-Building Strategies Matters:

1. Freedom and Flexibility: Financial independence provides freedom and flexibility to pursue passions, interests, and aspirations without being tied to a traditional job or career path.
2. Security and Stability: Wealth-building strategies create a solid financial foundation, providing security and stability against economic uncertainties, emergencies, and life transitions.
3. Legacy and Impact: Building wealth allows individuals to leave a legacy, support loved ones, and make a positive impact in their communities and the world at large.

Anecdotes of Financial Independence and Wealth-Building Strategies

The Early Retirement Enthusiast: Sarah, inspired by the concept of financial independence, embarked on a journey to achieve early retirement. She adopted a frugal lifestyle, saved aggressively, and invested prudently to build a sizable nest egg. By adhering to her wealth-building strategies and staying focused on her goal, Sarah achieved financial independence in her 40s, allowing her to retire early and pursue her passions and interests with confidence and freedom.

The Entrepreneurial Visionary: Mark, with a vision of building wealth through entrepreneurship, founded a successful startup in the tech industry. He identified market opportunities, assembled a talented team, and executed a strategic business plan to drive growth and profitability. Through perseverance, innovation, and strategic decision-making, Mark built a thriving business that generated substantial wealth, providing financial security for himself and his family while making a positive impact in the industry.

The Passive Income Investor: David, recognizing the power of passive income in achieving financial independence, focused on building multiple streams of income through investments in real estate, stocks, and other income-generating assets. He diversified his portfolio, minimized risk, and prioritized cash flow generation to create a sustainable income stream that supported his desired lifestyle. By leveraging passive income strategies, David achieved financial independence and gained the freedom to pursue his interests and passions on his own terms.

Strategies for Financial Independence and Wealth-Building

1. Set Clear Goals: Define your financial independence and wealth-building goals, outlining specific targets, timelines, and action plans for achieving them.

2. Adopt a Growth Mindset: Cultivate a growth mindset that embraces learning, adaptation, and resilience in the pursuit of financial independence and wealth accumulation.
3. Maximize Income: Explore opportunities to maximize income through career advancement, entrepreneurship, side hustles, and passive income strategies to accelerate wealth-building efforts.
4. Invest Wisely: Develop a diversified investment strategy that aligns with your risk tolerance, time horizon, and financial goals, focusing on long-term growth and wealth preservation.

Conclusion

Zeroing in on financial independence and wealth-building strategies is a transformative journey that requires vision, discipline, and perseverance. By setting clear goals, adopting prudent financial habits, and implementing strategic wealth- building strategies, individuals can achieve financial independence, build lasting wealth, and enjoy a life of freedom, security, and fulfillment. Remember, the path to financial independence is unique for each individual, and it requires dedication, patience, and a commitment to lifelong learning and growth.

CHAPTER 28

THE DIGITAL BATTLEFIELD - SCAMS, SCHEMES, AND THE POWER OF SENSE X©

*I*n today's hyper-connected world, your financial future is not just built by smart investments, savvy savings, and careful spending. It's also about navigating the digital landscape safely and securely. As technology has advanced, so too have the methods used by scammers and cybercriminals. From phishing emails to sophisticated social engineering schemes, the internet is a breeding ground for financial traps that can derail your financial journey in an instant. The saying that operates in this finternet jungle is "dont give a hungry man a fish, teach him phishing". But with the right mindset and tools—what I call "Sense X©"—you can fortify your defenses and secure your financial future.

The Anatomy of a Scam: Real-Life Examples

1. The Phishing Trap: A Simple Click Can Cost You Thousands

Consider the case of Sarah, a 35-year-old marketing manager who thought she was being cautious online. One day, she received an email that appeared to be from her bank. The email warned her that her account had been compromised and that she needed to verify her details immediately. The email looked legitimate, complete with the bank's logo and a professional tone. Without a second thought, Sarah clicked on the link and entered her login details. Within minutes, her account was emptied.

What Sarah didn't realize was that she had fallen victim to a phishing scam, where cybercriminals create fake emails and websites that look like they belong to trusted institutions. These scams prey on a sense of urgency and fear, pushing victims to act without thinking.

2. The Investment Fraud: Too Good to Be True

Then there's the story of Mark, an aspiring investor who was eager to grow his savings. Mark was approached online by someone claiming to be a financial advisor with an exclusive investment opportunity. The returns promised were astronomical—far higher than anything Mark had seen before. Excited by the potential, Mark invested a substantial amount of money, only to find out later that the so-called "advisor" had disappeared, along with his money.

This type of scam, known as an investment fraud or Ponzi scheme, often targets individuals who are looking to make quick money. The allure of high returns blinds the victim to the red flags, such as vague information about the investment, pressure to invest quickly, and the lack of verifiable credentials.

3. The Social Media Deception: Trust and Betrayal

In another incident, Jane, a university student, connected with a seemingly friendly individual on social media. Over time, they built a relationship, and Jane began to trust this person. Eventually, they convinced her to lend them a significant amount of money, promising to pay her back with interest. As soon as the money was sent, the person disappeared, blocking Jane on all platforms.

This is a classic example of a social engineering scam, where the scammer manipulates their victim into believing they are someone trustworthy. These scams often exploit emotions, making them particularly devastating.

Building Your Cyber Defense with Sense X©

So, how do you protect yourself from these and countless other online threats? The answer lies in developing your

Sense X©—a heightened awareness and instinct that goes beyond basic cyber hygiene.

1. Trust, but Verify

Sense X© starts with a simple principle: trust, but verify. In the digital world, things are not always what they seem. When you receive an email, message, or investment opportunity, take a moment to question its legitimacy. Verify the sender's identity, look for signs of phishing (such as grammatical errors, unusual URLs, or unexpected requests), and never click on links or download attachments from unknown sources. In the case of Sarah, a quick call to her bank would have revealed that the email was a scam.

2. Recognize Red Flags

Another key aspect of Sense X© is the ability to recognize red flags. Scammers often create a sense of urgency to push you into making hasty decisions. Whether it's an investment that seems too good to be true, a friend asking for money, or an unexpected message from your bank, always take a step back. Ask yourself: Does this make sense? Why would someone I barely know ask for money? Why is this investment opportunity so secretive? Mark's story highlights the importance of doing your own research before making any financial commitments.

3. Educate Yourself Continuously

The digital landscape is constantly evolving, and so are the tactics used by scammers. Staying informed is crucial. Follow cybersecurity news, take online courses, and engage in forums or groups that discuss online safety. By keeping up to date, you'll be better equipped to recognize new threats as they emerge.

4. Leverage Technology

While Sense X© is about developing your instincts, it's also about using the right tools. Leverage technology to build your defenses. Use multi-factor authentication (MFA) on all your accounts, enable alerts for unusual activity, and consider using a password manager to create and store complex passwords. Regularly update your software and devices to protect against the latest vulnerabilities. Had Jane used stronger security measures, she might have prevented her scammer from accessing her accounts in the first place.

5. Trust Your Gut

Finally, never underestimate the power of intuition. If something feels off, it probably is. Scammers often rely on their victims ignoring that nagging feeling that something isn't right. Your gut is an essential part of Sense X©—it's your internal alarm system. If you sense danger, it's better to be cautious and take the time to investigate.

Empowering Your Financial Future

The internet offers endless opportunities, but it also comes with risks. By cultivating your Sense X©, you can navigate the digital world with confidence, protecting your assets and securing your financial future. Remember, online safety isn't just about technology—it's about awareness, vigilance, and the ability to think critically in every situation. With Sense X©, you're not just reacting to threats; you're anticipating and neutralizing them before they can harm you.

In the context of Sense X©, the concept of Deception Management becomes essential in safeguarding your financial well-being. Just as "Sense X©" empowers you to tap into your intuitive abilities for financial growth, Deception Management equips you with a set of principles designed to shield you from the growing threats in today's digital landscape.

1. Disbelieve Exaggerated Claims: The first rule of Deception Management aligns perfectly with Sense X©. Just as Sense X© encourages skepticism and critical thinking, you should automatically disbelieve any claim of exaggerated returns on

investment (ROI). Your Sense X© should be attuned to spot these red flags.

2. Verify Identities: Sense X© sharpens your intuition, allowing you to sense when something is off. Apply this heightened awareness when receiving calls, especially from those claiming to represent banks or other institutions. Always verify the caller's identity before engaging.

3. Maintain Privacy: Your financial moves are personal, and so should your sense of privacy be. Sense X© teaches you the importance of keeping your financial strategies to yourself to avoid attracting predatory attention.

4. Beware of Technology: Sense X© isn't just about intuition; it's about being technologically savvy too. Be cautious about investing in schemes where the promoters are faceless entities. Use your Sense X© to investigate and validate before committing.

5. Protect Confidential Information: Sense X© is your inner shield. It should guide you to never share confidential information like passwords or PINs with anyone, even those who seem trustworthy.

6. Question Online Identities: In the world of social media and online interactions, your Sense X© should raise alarms when someone's online persona doesn't match their claims. Always question and verify.

7. **Manage Greed:** Sense X© helps you balance ambition with caution. Understand that fraudsters exploit greed. Curb your appetite for quick, excessive profits, and you'll be less vulnerable to scams. Always remember the saying that money is a good servant but a bad master and never allow it to rule your heart.

8. **Research Reputation:** Your Sense X© should prompt you to dig deeper. Before engaging with any person or organization, check their online reputation thoroughly.

9. **Segregate Bank Accounts:** Sense X© advocates for practical financial management. Keep your primary savings account separate from your gpay linked account to limit exposure to potential fraud.

10. **Be Wary of Close Recommendations:** Even those closest to you can unknowingly introduce you to fraudsters. Sense X© teaches you to trust but verify, even within your inner circle.

Incorporating these principles of Deception Management into your life complements the power of Sense X©, ensuring that you are not only financially successful but also secure in an increasingly deceptive world.

As you continue your journey to financial success, let Sense X© be your guide. Stay informed, stay aware, and most importantly, stay safe. Your financial future depends on it.

ANNEXURE

Measure Your Sense X©

Find your Sense X©:

Here's a questionnaire to assess financial intelligence:

1. Budgeting and Planning:
   - Do you create a monthly budget?
   - How often do you review and adjust your budget?
   - Do you set financial goals and milestones?

2. Investment Knowledge:
   - Are you familiar with different investment vehicles (stocks, bonds, mutual funds, etc.)?
   - Have you ever invested in stocks or other financial instruments?
   - How comfortable are you with assessing investment risks?

3. Debt Management:
   - Do you have a plan for paying off any existing debts?
   - How do you manage credit cards and other forms of debt?

- Have you ever consolidated debt or negotiated lower interest rates?

4. Savings Habits:
   - What percentage of your income do you save each month?
   - Do you have an emergency fund? If so, how many months' worth of expenses does it cover?
   - How do you prioritize saving for different financial goals (retirement, education, vacations, etc.)?

5. Financial Literacy:
   - How would you rate your understanding of basic financial concepts (interest rates, inflation, compounding, etc.)?
   - Do you actively seek out financial education resources (books, articles, courses, etc.)?
   - Have you ever sought professional financial advice?

Scoring:
- Assign points to each question based on the level of financial responsibility demonstrated.
- Higher points indicate greater financial intelligence.
- Tally up the scores to find the person's financial intelligence score.6. Financial Goal Setting: Do you have clearly defined short-term and

long-term financial goals? How often do you review and adjust your financial goals?

7. Budgeting and Tracking Expenses: Do you maintain a budget to track your income and expenses? How frequently do you track your expenses against your budget?

8. Debt Management: What percentage of your income goes towards debt repayment? Are you actively working to reduce or eliminate debt?

9. Savings and Investments: Do you have an emergency fund set aside for unexpected expenses? What percentage of your income do you save or invest regularly?

10. Financial Knowledge: How comfortable are you with basic financial concepts such as compound interest, inflation, and risk management? Do you actively seek out financial education resources to improve your knowledge?

11. Risk Management: Do you have insurance coverage for major risks such as health, property, and life? How diversified is your investment portfolio to mitigate risk?

12. Decision Making: Can you provide an example of a financial decision you made recently and how you arrived at that decision? How do you evaluate the

potential risks and rewards before making a financial decision?

13. Financial Discipline: How disciplined are you in sticking to your financial plan and avoiding impulsive purchases? Have you developed strategies to overcome any financial challenges or setbacks?

14. Future Planning: Do you have a retirement plan in place? How confident are you in your ability to achieve your financial goals in the future?

15. Continuous Improvement: Are you open to seeking professional financial advice or guidance when needed? Do you regularly review and adjust your financial strategies based on changes in your life circumstances or economic conditions?

16. Risk Tolerance in Market Volatility:

    How did you react to significant market downturns, such as the 2008 Global Financial Crisis or the COVID pandemic-induced market crash in 2022

    Did you panic and sell off investments, stay invested but felt anxious, or saw it as an opportunity to buy more?

    On a scale of 1 to 5, where 1 represents a high level of panic and selling, and 5 represents a calm and strategic approach to investing during market downturns, how would you rate your behavior?

By assessing how individuals react to market volatility and downturns, we can gauge their risk tolerance and ability to remain disciplined in their investment strategy during challenging economic conditions.

17. Giving to Charitable Causes:
    a. How frequently do you donate money to charitable organizations or good causes?
    b. What motivates you to donate to a particular cause or organization?
    c. How do you typically decide which charities or causes to support financially?
    d. What factors influence the amount of money you donate to a cause?
    e. Have you ever donated to a crowdfunding campaign for a social or environmental cause? If yes, what influenced your decision to donate?

Each question is scored on a scale (e.g., 1 to 5) based on the respondent's answers, and the total score provides an overall assessment of their financial intelligence.

Max score being 5 x 17 or 85 , find your percentage score by dividing your Sense X© score by 85 and multiplying by 100. For example, if your total score is 60, then your Sense X© is 70 percent.

TESTIMONIALS

$\mathcal{S}$ense X© is a groundbreaking concept that revolutionizes the way we approach personal finance. As a seasoned banker and financial expert, I can attest that this book offers a unique and innovative perspective on financial intelligence. The author's extensive experience and divine wisdom in combating economic crimes and scams shines through in this comprehensive guide, providing readers with practical tools to measure and develop their financial acumen. Whether you're a seasoned investor or just starting out, Sense X© is an essential read to help you navigate the complex world of finance with confidence. Get ready to unlock your financial potential and stay financially free and secure.

– PCR Suresh,
Risk Management Consultant & Former Senior Vice President of Standard Chartered Bank

I believe books have the power to influence your thinking in the conscious and unconscious mind. Sense X© is a masterclass in taking abstract concepts and turning them into actionable ideas. Dr Prateep V Philip combines practical insights with vivid imagination in delivering a playbook on finance that can benefit all mankind.

– Kumar Vaidyanathan,
Business Strategist, Melbourne

Technology is a blessing. But it can trap you if you do not understand how to master it. One of the most reported misuses of technology is in the financial sector with large number of scams where people end up losing millions. That is where financial intelligence comes in. Can we , the common people be financially intelligent? Yes, we can provided we learn from the right source. Dr Prateep V Philip IPS, PhD, the author of this book is the most appropriate person to help us learn about this brand new concept and keep our money safe and growing. He has had first hand experience of this heading the economic offences wing of the police. I encourage you to buy this book and learn from it. Secure your financial future. Learn from the best.

– Madana Kumar, PhD.,
Vice President-Leadership Development at UST,
Co-founder at Leadyne, Author and Coach,
Servant Leadership

Financial Literacy and Financial Intelligence or the lack of it is the biggest reason why human societies have been subjected in the past and in the modern world, to be an informed consumer. Dr Prateep Philip's book is an opportunity to learn and develop the importance of becoming financially intelligent and acquire the character of citizenship.

> **– Osama Manzar,**
> *Founder & Director,*
> *Digital Empowerment Foundation,*
> *the man who has travelled to more than*
> *10,000 villages to promote Digital Literacy*

Sense X© would be an excellent tool, refresher and ready to refer source for anyone and everyone. It would prove very useful for the young generation, with liquidity overhang and the resultant wasteful spending. It would be a timely reminder for those who are just in the initial years of family building - whether single income or double income. For the spendthrift generation, this would help apply the brakes, before they go into a tailspin and financial mess.

> **– Sukumar Samuel,**
> *Financial Consultant and Independent Director*

Financial literacy is important to avoid wrong financial decisions and choices. Dr. Prateep takes this even further with this book on Financial Intelligence. In this book, he has illustrated how practicing simple techniques in our day to day life can help in safeguarding and accumulating wealth. The anecdotal practical examples that Dr. Prateep has extensively used makes the reader to easily relate to their personal contexts. Wrong financial choices bring in despair and ruin, as we see in so many instances everyday. Sense X will help the readers to cultivate the right financial habits, which if practiced diligently, would lead to wealth creation.

– Thillai Rajan A.,
Professor, Department of Management Studies and Head, Centre for Research on Start-ups and Risk Financing, IIT Madras

OTHER BOOKS BY THE AUTHOR

Available on Amazon and other online book sites:

1. The Friends of Police Movement: A Roadmap for Proactive People Protection
2. Word Empowered Life - https://amzn.in/d/0A2AUTQ
3. For Better through Verse
4. Fillipisms 3333 Maxims to Maximize Your Life - https://amzn.in/d/5ee6g4A

To share feedback and to place bulk orders, contact author: prateep.philip@gmail.com

For more information, please refer to the following links:

www.prateepphilip.com
www.friendsofpolice.net
www.fillipisms.com

www.ingramcontent.com/pod-product-compliance
Lightning Source LLC
LaVergne TN
LVHW041844070526
838199LV00045BA/1432